THE STARS WITHIN YOU

THE STARS WITHIN YOU

A MODERN GUIDE TO ASTROLOGY

Juliana McCarthy

ILLUSTRATED BY ALEJANDRO CARDENAS

ROOST BOOKS
BOULDER
2018

Roost Books
An imprint of Shambhala Publications, Inc.
4720 Walnut Street
Boulder, Colorado 80301
roostbooks.com

9 8 7 6 5 4 3 2 1

First Edition
Printed in the United States of America

♾This edition is printed on acid-free paper that meets the
American National Standards Institute Z39.48 Standard.
♻Shambhala Publications makes every effort to print on recycled paper.
For more information please visit www.shambhala.com.

Roost Books is distributed worldwide by
Penguin Random House, Inc., and its subsidiaries.

Designed by Laura Shaw Design

Library of Congress Cataloging-in-Publication Data
Names: McCarthy, Juliana, author.
Title: The stars within you: a modern guide to astrology / Juliana McCarthy;
illustrations by Alejandro Cardenas.
Description: First Edition. | Boulder: Roost Books, 2018.
Identifiers: LCCN 2017050695 | ISBN 9781611805116 (pbk.: alk. paper)
Subjects: LCSH: Astrology.
Classification: LCC BF1708.1 .M33 2018 | DDC 133.5—dc23
LC record available at https://lccn.loc.gov/2017050695

CONTENTS

PREFACE

My first introduction to astrology came when I was eighteen years old. I was quiet and reserved, and I didn't really understand myself. Having been a dancer most of my life, I was comfortable onstage, but somehow I clammed up in social situations. The truth was, people perplexed me. Ever since I could remember, I felt like an alien, unable to understand the illogical world of human complexity—even within myself. One day, someone gave me an astrology book, and I began to look up all of my planets and their descriptions. I was amazed by the accuracy, and something began to click for me. Here was a logical system that could help me comprehend the confusing layers of life's contradictions.

My shyness was easy enough to understand. After all, my Sun and Ascendant are in coy, meek Virgo. Yet I am also terribly romantic, which makes sense because my Venus, planet of love, falls in amorous Libra. My Mars in Leo explains my ability to be onstage—my planet of physical exertion and confidence falls in the sign of entertainment and creative expression. As I continued to learn, I was able to apply these archetypes to others as well, and people actually started making sense. For the first time my mind began opening to magic and the possibility that life has invisible dimensions and auspicious synchronicities.

Suddenly, I had a golden key that was helping me to grasp human psychology, personality, and relationships, and I dove into my astrological studies with obsessive fervor. I looked up the planets of everyone around me, and I began to understand the energies of the planets and signs, their meaning, and how they manifested in the people I knew. Soon, I had learned enough to read charts, and I've been reading them ever since.

Years later, I found an astrology teacher in Boulder, Colorado. He helped me fill in the gaps, particularly the more complicated facets of astrology—like progressed charts and solar returns. That teacher was the wonderful Kelly Lee Phipps, whose mind was quick and almost inhumanly brilliant. He would talk fast, pulling together complex ideas, giggling, and interrupting with handstands. After a couple of years' studying together, Kelly was diagnosed with brain cancer and tragically died a few months later. During the period when he was dying, he told me that I was ready to become a professional astrologer. The timing of his message was potent, so I took the leap, hoping to carry forward his wisdom and legacy.

I love astrology so much—the art of reading energy maps, which tell the story of who we are through myths and archetypes. I love being a translator for people, helping to reveal their connection to the cosmos. It is beautiful to see people in their fullest potential without even knowing them. In turn, my clients feel that astrology validates what they already knew about themselves but didn't have the language to express. They find comfort in being seen and recognized, and in realizing that they are reflected in the stars. In this way, astrology helps us to accept ourselves more readily—both our gifts and our struggles. Since the feedback about who we are comes from planets, not people, it helps us face ourselves without defensiveness, owning and embracing every dimension of our intricate beings.

In parallel to my study of astrology, I've spent many years practicing and studying Buddhism under the teacher Sakyong Mipham Rinpoche. Inevitably, my spiritual viewpoint has informed how I interpret the stars. This would be true of anyone, whether Buddhist, atheist, or something else. However, in the end what I'm most interested in, and what seems to be most helpful in astrological interpretation, is finding where various spiritual, philosophical, and scientific outlooks converge. This is where we find universal truth.

When reading charts, it is helpful to begin from a sensitive and nuanced spiritual standpoint. For example, there is no such thing as a "bad" placement or aspect. Struggles exist to help us unlock our potentials, opening portals to vulnerability, tenderness, and empathy. This way, we can blend our talents with authenticity and humility, showing up for the world in more meaningful ways.

When approached more subtly, I find astrology to be a wonderful tool not only for self-awareness, but also for opening minds and connecting us with vastness. That our personalities and psychology are aptly reflected by planetary positions is mind-boggling. It has opened me, and many others, to the possibility that life is not as solid as we think—that there are more than just the three dimensions of space and one of time. This widens our scope and helps us become more present, without limiting beliefs blocking our perception. It also amplifies our curiosity about others, increasing compassion by deepening our understanding of human nature. Knowing that we all have struggles—and relating to them with more awareness—encourages acceptance of both ourselves and others.

My goal for this book is to pass along my love and fascination for astrology. While it may seem far-fetched or fantastical to some, I ask that you dive in and investigate for yourself. See if the descriptions of natal planets ring true for you and the people around you.

As you learn the art of astrology, I hope you unlock your deepest potential, becoming more of who you are. I hope you can help others to do the same by holding up this powerful and revealing celestial mirror.

May you enjoy your journey into the enchanted land of cosmic myths.

—JULIANA McCARTHY

THE STARS WITHIN YOU

INTRODUCTION

....

Astrology is a language. If you understand
this language, the sky speaks to you.
—DANE RUDHYAR

MYTHOLOGY is fundamental to being human. It makes sense of disparate feelings, erratic thoughts, and random events. Without stories, we might lose track of purpose, mindlessly stumbling through our lives. As an ancient practice of systemized mythology connected to the stars, astrology provides a map that helps us better navigate our lives, imbuing us with magic, meaning, and greater self-awareness.

Astrology is also a language. By learning the language of the sky, we can commune with planets and stars, discovering important messages about who we are. The stars are speaking to us—astrology teaches us how to listen.

I have often wondered how our nature could be so aptly revealed by cosmic synchronicities. After reading countless astrology charts, the power and usefulness of this practice have been proven to me again and again. Astrology provides continuity within life's unpredictability. It expands our consciousness, improves our relationships, and reveals the gifts we have to offer the world.

Astrology is so much more than our Sun sign. Many of us have only engaged with astrology to the extent of casually reading our horoscopes in the backs of newspapers and magazines. Here, we've learned that as Scorpios, we are "intense and manipulative"; as Virgos, we are "uptight and neurotic"; as Cancers, we are "moody and overly sensitive." How limited would we feel if we bought into these reductive, simplistic descriptions of who we are? Astrology is far more dimensional.

When looking at our birth chart—the map of the sky at the moment of our first breath—we discover that we have multiple planets in addition to our Sun and Moon. Each planet represents a different facet of our character, tendencies, and potentials. In learning about our planets, we can discover ourselves endlessly while uncovering how we can live our most fulfilled life.

What are our natural talents? Where do we continually face obstacles? What are the keys to unlocking our spiritual growth? Astrology helps us answer these questions and more. The myths, archetypes, and stories connected to our planetary positions help depict our soul—weaving together our personality and proclivities into a rich, deep tapestry.

While astrological studies are inexhaustible and vast, we have to begin somewhere. This book is a starting point, providing an introduction to the basic tenets of chart reading—the signs, planets, aspects, and houses. With these building blocks, we can learn about our nature according to the stars. By the end of this book, readers will know how to read a birth chart.

By reading our birth chart, we can learn how to make better use of our gifts, and make peace with our weaknesses. We can understand more about how we think, act, relate, and love. In short, chart reading reveals how to access meaning, satisfaction, acceptance, and joy. Our Sun sheds light on what brings us happiness and vitality; our Moon uncovers our deeper emotional nature and what brings us contentment; our Venus tells the story of our values and relationships; our Mars points to our drives and the energies that stimulate us. Astrology helps us engage fully in all of our potentials.

Here is a list of planets and their areas of influence in our lives:

PLANET	SYMBOL	AREA OF INFLUENCE
Sun	☉	Self, main concerns, vitality
Moon	☽	Emotions, instincts, habits
Mercury	☿	Communication, intellect, reason
Venus	♀	Love, beauty, art
Mars	♂	Action, desire, aggression
Jupiter	♃	Expansion, optimism, abundance
Saturn	♄	Restriction, pessimism, structure
Uranus	♅	Rebellion, eccentricity, upheaval
Neptune	♆	Imagination, dreams, delusions
Pluto	♇	Transformation, obsession, power

Knowing our planets helps us consciously provide each of them proper nourishment so we can become more of who we are, without ignoring any aspect of ourselves. If we know, for example, that our Sun falls in Libra, we can recognize our need to pursue the Libran qualities of beauty, romance, and peace in order to feel joyful and alive; if our Moon falls in Leo, we know that we need to feed our Leonine desires for regular affection and adulation in order to feel fulfilled; if our Mars is in Gemini, we know we will feel energized when engaging in social and intellectual pursuits.

Whatever our reasons for exploring astrology, it can become a powerful tool for self-discovery. As we learn this cosmic language and art, we can become our own guides, helping ourselves unearth our true nature. Astrology provides a link between the terrestrial world and the astral, the poetic and the scientific. We end up opening portals to wisdom and our soul as we play with this logical, ancient planetary system, beautifully interlaced with myth, stories, magic, and the power of divination.

THE HISTORY OF ASTROLOGY

Astrology is an ancient practice, originating more than two thousand years ago. In the second millennium BC, the Babylonians became the first to develop an organized system of astrology. Initially, they used it to predict the seasons and the weather. Later, it became a form of celestial divination.

In the fourth century BC, the Babylonians introduced astrology to the Greeks and it continued to evolve. After the Alexandrian conquests of Egypt around the late second or early first century BC, Babylonian and Egyptian Decanic astrology merged. The combination became known as Hellenistic astrology, which was *horoscopic*, including an Ascendant and twelve celestial houses, just like we use today. The focus moved toward the individual's birth chart and the interpretation of the planetary positions at the time of birth.

Hellenistic astrology quickly spread across the ancient world, into Europe and the Middle East. The great philosophers and scientists of the day began to study astrology, and it soon became a highly regarded science, inseparable from astronomy. In fact, many legendary scientists and philosophers were astrologers, including Copernicus, Galileo, Kepler, and Sir Isaac Newton. They considered it to be a science of the soul.

Astrology took a downward turn during the Age of Enlightenment, when scientific materialism began to dominate philosophical thought. People were placing more and more emphasis on what was tangible, solid, and provable, rather than the esoteric. Astrology fell by the wayside, into the category of superstition and nonsense. However, it never quite died out. Despite its many critics, astrology has survived throughout the ages.

In the twentieth century, pioneering astrologers, such as Dane Rudhyar and Charles Carter, began reformulating astrology, finding it to be helpful in understanding our psyche, personality, character, and innate potentials. The tone began shifting away from the fatalism and moralism historically present in astrology, toward more sophisticated spiritual and psychological understanding. The notion that we have free will, that our lives and personalities are fluid and changeable, became the cornerstone of contemporary astrology. It began to be recognized as a powerful means of self-discovery.

Carl Jung, the highly regarded founder of analytical psychology, also greatly contributed to astrology's resurgence and reformulation. He gleaned much of his psychological understanding from his astrological studies. In a letter to Sigmund Freud in 1911, he wrote:

At the moment I am looking into astrology, which seems indispensable for a proper understanding of mythology. There are strange and wondrous things in these lands of darkness. Please, don't worry about my wanderings in these infinitudes. I shall return laden with rich booty for our knowledge of the human psyche.

Jung's explorations into astrology were fruitful. He helped illuminate the importance of archetypes and myth in the process of knowing ourselves and healing our psyches. He believed archetypal symbols were the language of the soul and that our birth charts provided maps of who we are. Jung even looked at patients' astrological charts in difficult cases. In a 1947 letter to Hindu astrologer B.V. Raman, Jung wrote:

In cases of difficult psychological diagnosis I usually get a horoscope in order to have a further point of view from an entirely different angle. I must say that I very often found that the astrological data elucidated certain points which I otherwise would have been unable to understand.

The correlations were so strong between patients and their charts that Jung was often able to learn more about his patients' minds from their birth charts than from witnessing them firsthand. Jung's wanderings into psychology, astrology, and myth shaped modern-day astrology. Psychological astrology became the dominant astrological movement in the twentieth century, springing from Jung's influence. To this day, many important astrologers continue to reference Jung as important reading material for astrological studies.

Later in the twentieth century, astrology experienced a surge in popularity during the cultural revolution of the sixties—a time when many became interested in practices of Eastern philosophy and ancient wisdom. By the seventies, astrology had become an integral part of mainstream culture, with horoscopes appearing in major newspapers and magazines. At this time, the question, "What's your sign?" became part of our everyday vernacular.

Today, astrology seems to be more popular than ever. There are close to ten million astrologers working in the United States, over two million websites that mention astrology, and an increasing number of universities including astrology in their curricula. Having captured the minds and hearts of many intelligent and deep thinkers, astrology has proven to be a powerful tool of awareness and an insightful means for understanding human nature and psychology. The celestial myths and archetypes have shown themselves to be universal and true, having resonated for millennia.

The cosmos is a vast living body, of which we are still parts.
The Sun is a great heart whose tremors run through our smallest veins.
The Moon is a great nerve center from which we quiver forever.
Who knows the power that Saturn has over us, or Venus? But it is a
vital power, rippling exquisitely through us all the time.
—D. H. LAWRENCE

THE BASICS

The basic building blocks of astrology that are necessary for reading charts are the planets, signs, houses, and aspects. The **planets** tell us which human energies we are working with; the **signs** tell us how these energies manifest; the **houses** tell us where we direct these energies, or the area of life toward which we apply them; and the **aspects**, or angles, tell us how these energies relate to each other within us.

Before we go further, it is important to understand that each of us has a Sun, Moon, and Ascendant, along with eight additional planets. Our birth chart consists of a zodiac wheel divided into twelve houses, which represent different facets of life—such as money, relationship, career, and spirituality. Our planets fall at various degrees within our chart, each in a different house. Earth is always implied in the middle of our chart, and where the planets fall within the 360° zodiac wheel depicts their positions relative to Earth.

The first step to engaging with this book is to find a copy of your birth chart. Many websites generate charts for free if you type in your birth date, time, and location. The best site for this is astro.com. Once you have a copy of your chart and know which signs your planets fall into, you can begin to dive into this book, looking up the meaning of each of your placements.

On the next page is an example of a birth chart, so you can see the lay of the land. Right now, this may look like random lines and indecipherable symbols, but by the end of this book, you will have the tools necessary to interpret their meaning. You will be able to understand the language of astrology—of symbols, angles, and myths. And you will be able to apply this understanding to yourself and others who you're interested in knowing more about. Keep in mind that the study of astrology is endless and ongoing. We could spend our whole lives studying astrology and still find more to learn—with countless perspectives, methods, and discoveries that continue to refine our understanding.

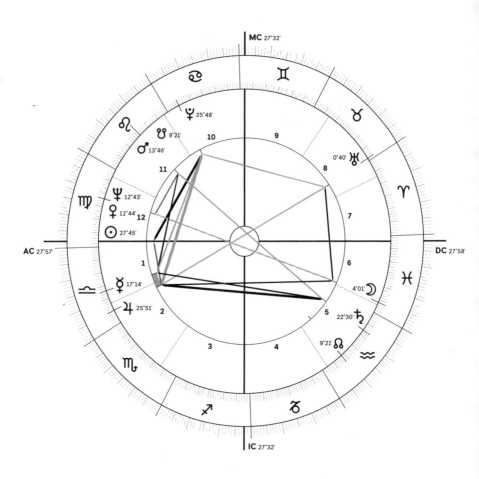

LEONARD COHEN'S BIRTH CHART

Aries	Taurus	Gemini	Cancer
Leo	Virgo	Libra	Scorpio
Sagittarius	Capricorn	Aquarius	Pisces

After you look up your chart, you can refer to this list of the signs and their symbols to help you determine where your planets fall in your chart. (You may also refer to the planetary symbols in the chart on page 3).

AN INTUITIVE ART

As we learn the art of astrology, it is important to drop into our intuitive minds, reflecting on the archetypes—feeling into them rather than thinking about them intellectually. For example, knowing that Gemini is social, communicative, and intellectual, we could try contemplating that from our hearts, feeling how that energy manifests within us. How do we feel when we're operating primarily from our minds—when we're curious, talkative, and speedy? Or in considering Venus, the planet of love, romance, luxury, and aesthetics, we can once again drop into our hearts and notice what it feels like to touch in with our romantic nature and our love of beauty and art. Here, we connect with Venus directly and intuitively.

Once we're comfortable with our impressions of these energies, we can hold them up to another person. For example, in relating to Taurus, we could start by considering the main qualities of this sign—sensual, earthy, and careful. After contemplating these traits, feeling how they manifest within ourselves, we could find someone we know, or someone famous, who has dominant Taurus in her chart. How does this person come across? Does she embody the slow and sensual Taurean traits? Similarly, how does someone with dominant Mars (or Mars-ruled Aries) in his chart feel? Does he seem impassioned, impulsive, and confident, demonstrating his Marsian qualities in obvious ways? This is how we can begin to embark on the fun and illuminating path of intuitive astrological exploration, governed by experience—rather than simply studying and memorizing facts.

The rich images in this book (created by the talented artist Alejandro Cardenas) are here to help us connect more viscerally to the astrological archetypes and energies. As you move through the book, I recommend spending time with the images. See how they line up with the descriptions of the signs. Allow them to permeate your nonthinking mind.

For example, looking at the image of Capricorn (page 54), what do you notice? Capricorn is represented by a goat's torso with a fish's tail. What does the depiction of this combination evoke in you? What feelings or associations arise when considering the steady goat who gradually climbs the mountain, one foot in front of the other and who also dives into the ocean's depths? Perhaps this represents an ability to connect with the fluid realms of emotions and spirituality, while also harnessing pragmatism and earthly abilities. Compare the description of Capricorn to the image and see what you notice, see what you feel. Being able to connect with our intuitive minds in these ways—with the broader brushstrokes of nonintellectual feeling and observation—is important to learning the art of astrology; it is equal parts systematic and intuitive.

THE BIG PICTURE

As we understand the various dimensions of astrology and weave together the cosmic tapestry of who we are, we have at our disposal an insightful and logical framework to help us make sense of our illogical selves. After all, we are multilayered beings with complexities and contradictions. We can be restrained in certain situations and wild and free in others. We could need tremendous emotional security and also require significant amounts of adventure and spontaneity. Rather than feel anxious or confounded by our paradoxes, we could shine light on these rich layers—calling on astrology to understand them better. This way, we could approach ourselves and each other with increased awareness, compassion, and objectivity.

As astrology grows in mainstream popularity, this timeless art has the potential to further our wisdom. It can help us develop more tolerance, depth, and humor so we can find meaning and connection, and grow more fully into our truest selves. We can better appreciate our strengths while embracing our challenges with humility. From there, we could discover our true purpose. What are our gifts, and how can we offer them to the world in joyful and meaningful ways?

As you begin to learn this mystical and practical art, keep in mind the notion presented in the preface, that there are no bad aspects or placements in astrology. Where we struggle becomes our opening to healing, empathy, and the desire to help each other. In other words, our pain can be our biggest gift.

As always, it is up to us what we do with our potentials. As the saying goes, the stars incline, they do not compel. Our lives are ultimately governed by our own free will.

1

THE SIGNS

The Twelve Archetypes of Personality

THE TWELVE SIGNS of the zodiac are the foundation of astrology, representing the archetypes, or personalities, present in human nature. Ripe with symbols, myths, and images, the signs unlock our journey of self-discovery. While most of us know our Sun sign (discussed in chapter 2), our personalities actually include all twelve of the zodiac signs. Some hold more weight for us than others, depending on the planetary positions at the moment we were born. For example, if many of our planets fall in Cancer, that sign would be more dominant in our personality. With no planets in Capricorn, our Capricornian traits might be hidden or underdeveloped.

THE ZODIAC

To grasp the signs of the zodiac fully, it helps to first understand what exactly the *zodiac* means. The zodiac is an oblong circle spanning the sky, extending 8° above and below the *ecliptic*, or the Sun's path from the perspective of Earth. This circle includes the orbits of all the planets moving around the Sun, except for Pluto, which has an exceptionally

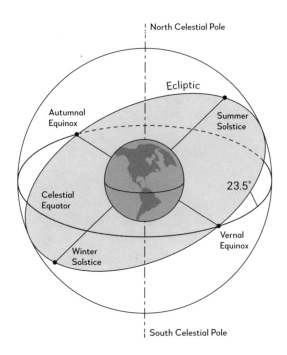

North Celestial Pole

Ecliptic

Autumnal
Equinox

Summer
Solstice

23.5°

Celestial
Equator

Vernal
Equinox

Winter
Solstice

South Celestial Pole

wide path. Also contained in the zodiac are the stars visible from Earth. In ancient times, people found that the shapes formed by the brightest stars resembled animals. This is why the circle of constellations became known as the zodiac, stemming from the Greek word *zodiakos*, meaning "circle of animals."

In astrology, our birth chart consists of a zodiac wheel, or a perfect 360° circle that represents the ecliptic. This is divided into twelve signs that are about 30° each. The signs roughly correspond with the constellations, with Aries located at the Spring Equinox, Cancer at the Summer Solstice, Libra at the Fall Equinox, and Capricorn at the Winter Solstice.

The signs of the zodiac have names and corresponding animals or figures, which were assigned by ancient astrologers based on the constellations. Each sign and constellation also has a story, which has been passed down over thousands of years through ancient mythology. These myths continue to inform our understanding of the astrological archetypes.

Winter
Solstice

WINTER

Capricorn Sagittarius

FALL

Aquarius

Scorpio

Pisces

Libra

Spring
Equinox

Fall
Equinox

Aries

Virgo

Taurus

Leo

SPRING

Gemini Cancer

SUMMER

Summer
Solstice

LEARNING THE SIGNS

Learning the signs is the best entry point into astrological study, since they apply to all other areas of chart reading. We each have a Sun, Moon, Ascendant, and eight additional planets, all of which fall into different signs that reveal layers of our distinct personalities. To understand the placement of any of our planets, we must first become familiar with the signs—deepening our understanding of their unique energies and characteristics.

The signs operate in a cyclical pattern. We begin our journey with Aries, the trailblazer and baby of the zodiac; then we move into Taurus, who unleashes our body; Gemini, who unlocks our intellect; Cancer, who connects us with emotion; and Leo, who reveals our creative expression. The signs become increasingly more complex until we end with Pisces, who represents spirituality, transcendence, and oneness. As the final sign, Pisces encompasses all the signs that came before. After Pisces, we jump back into our bodies and begin again with Aries—sign of birth, freshness, and spring.

DUALITIES, TRIPLICITIES, AND QUADRUPLICITIES

There are three significant groupings of the signs, which help us better understand them. First, there are dualities, with each sign categorized as either masculine or feminine. Masculine signs are direct, outgoing, and energetic, while feminine signs are more receptive and self-contained.

MASCULINE	FEMININE
Aries	Taurus
Gemini	Cancer
Leo	Virgo
Libra	Scorpio
Sagittarius	Capricorn
Aquarius	Pisces

Then, we divide the signs according to their **elements** and **qualities**— also known as **triplicities** and **quadruplicities**. The **elements** (or triplicities), are **fire**, **earth**, **air**, and **water**. Fire signs are enthusiastic, spontaneous, and inspiring (Aries, Leo, Sagittarius). Earth signs are stable, slow, and pragmatic (Taurus, Virgo, Capricorn). Air signs are intellectual, social, and communicative (Gemini, Libra, Aquarius); and water signs are sensitive, intuitive, and emotional (Cancer, Scorpio, Pisces).

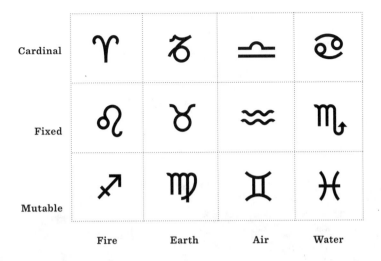

	Fire	Earth	Air	Water
Cardinal	♈	♑	♎	♋
Fixed	♌	♉	♒	♏
Mutable	♐	♍	♊	♓

The **qualities** (or quadruplicities) represent the three basic conditions in life—creation, preservation, and transformation. **Cardinal** signs are connected with creation and the beginning of each season (Aries, Cancer, Libra, and Capricorn). The **fixed** signs embody qualities of preservation, stability, and dependability. They mark the midpoint of each season (Taurus, Leo, Scorpio, and Aquarius). **Mutable** signs have to do with transformation—flexibility, change, and adaptability—and they show up at the end of each season (Gemini, Virgo, Sagittarius, and Pisces).

From here, we will examine each sign, unpacking the zodiacal journey. Covered in the following pages are each sign's ruling planet, symbol, and corresponding Greek myth. Take your time to contemplate the images, descriptions, and stories. They are here to open our intuitive minds, which is essential to chart reading. Also included are less traditional zodiacal elements, such as colors and crystals. These can further unlock our understanding of each sign, grounding the concepts into earthly metaphors.

ARIES

THE LEADER

RULING PLANET	Mars, Planet of Sexuality and Aggression
SYMBOL	The Ram
MAIN DESCRIPTORS	Courageous / Headstrong
DUALITY	Masculine
ELEMENT	Fire
QUALITY	Cardinal
KEYWORD	I AM
BODY PARTS	Head, Face, Adrenals, Blood
COLOR	Red, the Color of Passion
CRYSTALS	Bloodstone, Aventurite, Diamond
ATTRIBUTES	Willful, Aggressive, Enthusiastic, Innocent, Independent, Direct
INTERESTS	Hunting, Risk Taking, Fencing, Racing, Competition
DRIVE	To Trail-Blaze

PROGRESSION AND PLANET

As the first sign of the zodiac, Aries represents the start of the mythological journey through the stars. Aries also represents the beginning of the seasons and the energy of vitality—of baby animals and the first shoots of spring. The final sign of the zodiac is Pisces, which is all-encompassing, spiritual, and spacey. When we return to Aries, we are leaping back into our bodies, starting over with freshness, newness, and simplicity. Ruled by Mars, planet of physical exertion, Aries' energy is boundless. He leads others with courage, blazing trails without second thought.

SYMBOL

Symbolized by the Ram, Aries charges his opponents, unafraid of butting heads. While sheep are passive, rams can be dominant and even dangerous. Aries' fearlessness is unparalleled, as he bounds into uncharted territories, the rest of us following suit. His energy can sometimes manifest as directness, as he speaks his mind without hesitation. While his brazen honesty can offend, it comes from a place of genuineness and innocence. He is often unaware of the feelings he has hurt. This simplicity and straightforwardness is part of Aries' charm.

MYTH

The myth most associated with Aries is the Greek story of Phrixus and Helle, children of King Athamas. Their stepmother, Ino, hated them and tried to have them killed by hatching a devious plan. Right before their murder, a magical Ram flew in to save them, sent by their natural mother Nephele. The Ram took off with the children on his back, bringing them to safety. Afterward, Zeus placed a Ram's image in the heavens to immortalize his courage. The Ram then shed his golden fleece, which continued to be a source of inspiration and legend. From the sky, Aries the Ram now symbolizes leadership and bravery, along with the protective powers of his fabled golden fleece.

TAURUS

THE SENSUALIST

April 20–May 20

RULING PLANET	Venus, Planet of Love and Beauty
SYMBOL	The Bull
MAIN DESCRIPTORS	Dependable / Materialistic
DUALITY	Feminine
ELEMENT	Earth
QUALITY	Fixed
KEYWORD	I HAVE
BODY PARTS	Throat, Neck, Jaw, Larynx
COLOR	Green, the Color of Earth
CRYSTALS	Carnelian, Jade, Emerald
ATTRIBUTES	Stable, Patient, Elegant, Resourceful, Security-Oriented, Decadent
INTERESTS	Gardening, Dancing, Beautification, Yoga, Sensual Arts
DRIVE	To Luxuriate

PROGRESSION AND PLANET

Taurus moves us away from the impulsivity of Aries, teaching us to slow down and connect with our bodies. While Aries emboldens us, Taurus demonstrates stillness and silence. Along with Libra, Taurus is one of two signs ruled by Venus, planet of beauty and love. She aligns with the height of spring, when flowers are in bloom, filling the Northern Hemisphere with richness. When Venus returns to her command in Libra, the leaves change, and the world once again explodes with color. Representing the earthier sides of Venus, Taurus relishes in pleasure, prioritizing material security and sensual love.

SYMBOL

Symbolized by the Bull, Taurus is slow and stubborn, her head facing downward, toward the earth. A large and sturdy animal, the Bull's body is weighted to the ground through her enormity and the force of gravity. Moving slowly and steadily, Taurus takes her time to open her heart to vulnerability. When she does, her power is evident. She awakens our senses, connecting us to our bodies and the virtues of earthly delight.

MYTH

The Greek myth of Taurus comes from the story of Cerus, a large and powerful Bull, owned by no one. The spring goddess Persephone found him one day, trampling a field of flowers without realizing it. Although the Bull could not speak, he understood Persephone, and she calmed him by her very presence. Persephone taught the Bull patience and how to manage his strength. Every year thereafter, she and Cerus would reunite in early spring. Riding on top of him, they would set the flowers in bloom. When Persephone descends into Hades in the fall, Taurus returns to the night sky as a constellation. There, he reminds us of quiet steadiness, loyalty, and earthly splendor.

GEMINI

THE INTELLECTUAL

May 21–June 20

RULING PLANET	Mercury, Planet of Communication and Intellect
SYMBOL	The Twins
MAIN DESCRIPTORS	Intelligent / Unreliable
DUALITY	Both Feminine and Masculine
ELEMENT	Air
QUALITY	Mutable
KEYWORD	I THINK
BODY PARTS	Arms, Hands, Shoulders, Lungs, Nervous System
COLOR	Yellow, the Color of Illumination
CRYSTALS	Agate, Citrine, Sapphire
ATTRIBUTES	Communicative, Witty, Adaptable, Synergistic, Mischievous, Fickle
INTERESTS	Debating, Reading, Comedy, Tennis, Gossiping
DRIVE	To Gather Knowledge

PROGRESSION AND PLANET

Gemini arrives just after Taurus, helping us to raise our focus from the body to our minds so we can master intellect. Ruled by Mercury, planet of communication, Gemini moves quickly, darting from one subject to the next. He gathers information in order to broaden his knowledge and share it with others. A trickster who is ever curious, Gemini is prone to being deceptive and troublemaking, but only if his heart is closed. With pure intention, Gemini is a skillful teacher, revealing wisdom through eloquence and his sharpness of mind.

SYMBOL

Symbolized by the Twins, Gemini is notorious for having two sides or personalities, and for being two-faced. His dual nature lends to adaptability, as he's able to explore all facets of ideas or situations. Accumulating many friends and acquaintances, exchange is important for the Twins, who love to teach others, while trading ideas and quips. They are inquisitive, but also restless, with active minds that seldom rest.

MYTH

According to Greek myth, the Gemini Twins represent the brothers Castor and Pollux. Young and adventurous, they shared their life together with curiosity and zeal. Castor was mortal, Pollux immortal, and eventually Castor died, leaving Pollux distraught. Pollux went to his father, Zeus, and begged him to help. Zeus allowed Pollux to share his immortality with Castor, transforming them into the constellation Gemini so they could live together forever. From the sky, the Twins remind us of human complexity, as they embody mortality and divinity, separation and unity.

♋

CANCER

THE FEELER

June 21–July 22

RULING PLANET	The Moon, Which Rules Emotion
SYMBOL	The Crab
MAIN DESCRIPTORS	Sensitive / Moody
DUALITY	Feminine
ELEMENT	Water
QUALITY	Cardinal
KEYWORD	I FEEL
BODY PARTS	Breasts and Stomach
COLOR	Silver, the Color of the Moon
CRYSTALS	Moonstone, Silver, Pearl
ATTRIBUTES	Nurturing, Moody, Maternal, Empathetic, Family-Oriented, Clinging
INTERESTS	Cooking for Friends, Volunteering, Long Baths, Staying Home, Collecting
DRIVE	To Nurture

PROGRESSION AND PLANET

Cancer furthers our journey from Gemini's intellect into the realm of emotions. This feminine sign is highly sensitive and perceptive. Ruled by the Moon, which represents nurturing, feelings, and motherhood, Cancer feels deeply and loves to care for others. Watery and moody, she changes like the tides, feeling the pull of invisible forces. She is the archetypal mother, naturally receptive, deep, and imaginative, nourishing her loved ones. She is often successful working with the public, adjusting according to the moods and energies before her with exceptional intuition and subtlely.

SYMBOL

Symbolized by the Crab, Cancer carries her home on her back. This gives her great strength on the exterior while sometimes preventing her from revealing her softer interior. Pincers can come out, protecting her from the pain of deep sensitivity and vulnerability. With near psychic ability, she can feel what others are feeling. Her shell helps to form a barrier that delineates herself from others. Home is very important to the tender Crab, who needs a lot of alone time in coziness and comfort in order to regenerate. When she feels safe, no one is more caring than the Crab, who dances with loved ones in the sea of emotion, extending a visceral sense of home and sanctuary to anyone close to her.

MYTH

According to Greek myth, Cancer was a giant Crab named Crios, who guarded the sea nymphs of Poseidon's kingdom. He was enormous and immortal, and took his role of protector very seriously. One day, a few sea nymphs escaped, and Crios sent a giant squid named Vamari to retrieve them. The squid devoured them instead, and when he returned, Crios fought him to the death. Afterward, the Crab was crippled and in terrible pain. To repay him for his heroism, Poseidon relieved Crios of his pain by placing him in the sky as the constellation Cancer. From the sky, Cancer reminds us of the dear Crab's protectiveness, care, and vulnerable strength.

$\mathcal{\Omega}$

LEO

THE PERFORMER

July 23–August 22

RULING PLANET	The Sun, Which Rules Ego and Self-Expression
SYMBOL	The Lion
MAIN DESCRIPTORS	Expressive / Egoic
DUALITY	Masculine
ELEMENT	Fire
QUALITY	Fixed
KEYWORD	I WILL
BODY PARTS	Heart and Back
COLOR	Gold, the Color of the Sun
CRYSTALS	Onyx, Gold, Ruby
ATTRIBUTES	Warm, Loyal, Proud, Dramatic, Radiant, Fierce
INTERESTS	Performing, Sunbathing, Cuddling, Fund-Raising, Playing
DRIVE	To Impress

PROGRESSION AND PLANET

Leo continues the zodiac's progression from Cancer's sensitivity and emotionalism to a more extroverted expression and playfulness. Ruled by the Sun, Leo is heart-centered and warm, comfortable with others revolving around him. Like the Sun's powerful rays, Leo's creative self-expression is bright and limitless. He fearlessly extends his loyalty and joy to whoever is around him. Identifying so strongly with the sun, the center of our galaxy, Leo must only be wary of falling into self-absorption.

SYMBOL

Symbolized by the Lion, Leo is strong and confident, roaring freely as he displays the shock of his golden mane. Loving and lovable, the regal Lion prefers being king or queen, ruling with immeasurable compassion. If his ego grows too large, the Lion can fall off-kilter, operating from pride, vanity, and conceit, rather than his innate kindness. Cuddly and affectionate, the Lion can be a loving partner and friend, delighted when others bask in his light.

MYTH

According to Greek mythology, Leo was a mythical monster known as the Nemean Lion. Heracles was required to kill this Lion as one of his twelve labors—thought to be an impossible feat. Since the Lion was impervious to weapons, cunning Heracles eventually succeeded by strangling the Lion with his bare hands. Realizing the protective powers of the Lion's hide, Heracles skinned the Lion, making a cloak and helmet out of his fur and head. Then the spirit of the Lion was placed in the sky as the constellation Leo, reminding us of the Lion's mythic power and magical strength.

♍

VIRGO

THE HELPER

August 23–September 22

RULING PLANET	Mercury, Planet of Communication and Intellect
SYMBOL	The Virgin
MAIN DESCRIPTORS	Thoughtful / Judgmental
DUALITY	Feminine
ELEMENT	Earth
QUALITY	Mutable
KEYWORD	I ANALYZE
BODY PART	Intestines
COLOR	Blue, the Color of Calming
CRYSTALS	Carnelian, Amazonite, Sapphire
ATTRIBUTES	Organized, Logical, Health-Oriented, Devoted, Humble, Perfectionistic
INTERESTS	Caring for Animals, Editing, Writing, Organizing, Nutrition
DRIVE	To Serve Others

PROGRESSION AND PLANET

Virgo progresses from Leo's showiness to an orientation toward humility and serving others. Ruled by Mercury, planet of intelligence and communication, Virgo is a wordsmith like Mercury's other sign, Gemini. However, Virgo demonstrates a more careful style than Gemini, as well as detail-oriented perfectionism. Ever the analyzer, Virgo's intelligence can sometimes spin into stories and criticism. However, her loyalty is unparalleled. She readily applies her clear logic to solving problems and supporting others in need.

SYMBOL

Represented by the Virgin, one of Virgo's key traits is her love of purity. With loyalty and pure intentions, she devotes herself to caring for friends and even strangers, softening her sometimes-icy exterior once someone has earned her trust. At that point, Virgo can emerge as affectionate, gentle, magical, and warm. In Latin, the word *Virgo* means "self-contained," which is perhaps more accurate in depicting this sign than the literal virgin. Self-sufficient, Virgo devotes herself to serving the earth and all beings by first taking care of herself. She will continue working hard to benefit others, as long as she receives proper respect and appreciation.

MYTH

Astraea is perhaps the most interesting Greek goddess associated with Virgo. She was the last of the celestial beings to leave Earth at the start of the Bronze Age, after witnessing the degeneration of mankind. Goddess of innocence and purity, Astraea was a virgin and caretaker of humanity. When she left Earth, she was placed in the heavens as the Virgo constellation. Many believe that the adjacent Libra constellation represents Astraea's scales of justice. Shining from the sky, Virgo reminds us of virtue, as she waits to return to Earth in angelic form, as the ambassador of a new golden age.

LIBRA

THE ROMANTIC

September 23–October 22

RULING PLANET	Venus, Planet of Love and Beauty
SYMBOL	The Scales
MAIN DESCRIPTORS	Romantic / Indecisive
DUALITY	Masculine
ELEMENT	Air
QUALITY	Cardinal
KEYWORD	I BALANCE
BODY PARTS	Buttocks, Pancreas, and Kidneys
COLOR	Pink, the Color of Romance
CRYSTALS	Opal, Pink Tourmaline, Rose Quartz
ATTRIBUTES	Fair, Collaborative, Tasteful, Indecisive, Tactful, Refined
INTERESTS	Romance, Music Concerts, Museums, Songwriting, Making Art
DRIVE	To Love and Be Loved

PROGRESSION AND PLANET

Libra progresses from the austerity and criticality of Virgo to qualities of charm, romance, partnership, and artistry. When Libra arrives, his ruling planet Venus displays her overwhelming splendor. Leaves turn to brilliant colors in the Northern Hemisphere—to the oranges, reds, and yellows of early fall. In fact, Libra produces aesthetic allure in all that he touches, inspiring balance and serenity in artistic endeavors, relationships, and social gatherings. He is the most likely to come home with exquisite flowers, decorate his home with sensitivity and flair, and whisper sweet nothings to those he loves.

SYMBOL

Symbolized by the Scales, Libra represents justice and equilibrium. Taking his time to make decisions, Libra can become stagnant as he weighs both sides of every issue. Libra's opposite, Aries, is decisive but crude, while Libra is refined and polite, though often held back by hesitancy. Seeking to keep the Scales in balance, Libra demonstrates his diplomacy, elegance, and grace, enveloping friends and partners in magnanimity and appreciation. Despite his wishy-washy nature, Libra can be a crusader, possessing an unyielding sense of fairness. He can delicately stand up for what is right, balancing whatever is unjust or off-kilter.

MYTH

The main Libra myth revolves around the Greek goddess Astraea, represented by the constellation Virgo. Astraea was the goddess of innocence and purity who lived on Earth as a celestial being. She eventually fled, escaping the onslaught of human depravity, which appeared at the dawn of the Bronze Age. Astraea represented justice, just like her mother, Themis, the goddess of divine justice. When Zeus placed Astraea in the sky, she was holding the scales of justice, represented by the constellation Libra. The Libra Scales remind us of harmony, delicacy, and fairness. They help Astraea to hold her place in the sky, until the day she returns to Earth as the ruler of a new golden age.

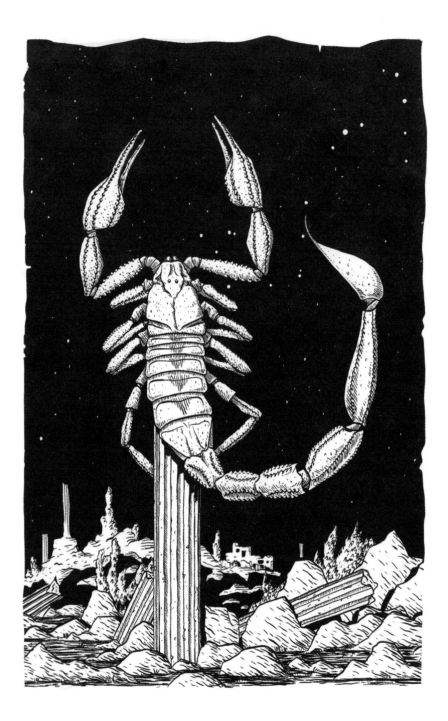

♏

SCORPIO

THE SHAMAN

October 23–November 21

RULING PLANETS	Mars and Pluto, Planets of Sexuality and Power
SYMBOL	The Scorpion
MAIN DESCRIPTORS	Passionate / Destructive
DUALITY	Feminine
ELEMENT	Water
QUALITY	Fixed
KEYWORD	I CREATE
BODY PARTS	Reproductive Organs
COLOR	Black, the Color of Mystery
CRYSTALS	Turquoise, Labradorite, Topaz
ATTRIBUTES	Intimate, Mysterious, Magnetic, Powerful, Intense, Obsessive
INTERESTS	Investigation, Science, Psychology, Tinkering, Magic
DRIVE	To Transform

PROGRESSION AND PLANET

Scorpio represents a shift into the more internal signs, which correlate with colder weather and seasons of introspection. We are moving away from Libra's niceties and small talk into Scorpio's urge to face unpleasant truths for the sake of intimacy. Pluto and Mars rule Scorpio, representing the process of death and rebirth, destruction and transformation. As the most extreme and mysterious sign, Scorpio is not afraid to dive into the depths. She readily plunges into intensity, alchemically transforming challenges into spiritual wisdom. Mars and Pluto are commanding and possessive planets, and Scorpio's ultimate spiritual attainment is to master the art of surrender. If she fails, she could find herself caught in fixation or emotional anguish. Representing the mastery of letting go, no sign has more of a transformational effect. After all, Scorpio is the shaman, possessing qualities of the mystic and psychologist, who help to heal our deepest wounds by holding our hand as we face our darkness with the light of awareness.

SYMBOL

The classic symbol for Scorpio is the Scorpion. However, two other symbols also represent Scorpio—the Eagle and the Phoenix. These three symbols embody the various layers of Scorpio's spiritual growth. When overwhelmed by challenging emotions, the Scorpion crawls on the ground, hiding away in dark corners of repression, ready to sting and destroy when threatened. The Eagle, too, can strike at any moment. But unlike the Scorpion, he glides through the sky—confident, visible, and free. The soaring bird has probing eyes, aware of subtleties that others might miss. The Phoenix is the most evolved of the symbols, representing the transformational quality of Scorpio as a mythological bird who cyclically regenerates. Dying in flames, the Phoenix is reborn from the ashes—life forming from destruction. Similarly, Scorpio's power comes from her willingness to open fully to fear, and to find spiritual rebirth from the little deaths of ego.

MYTH

The Greek myth most associated with Scorpio involves the god Orion and the goddess Artemis. One day, Orion bragged that he was the greatest hunter who existed and would kill every creature on earth to prove it. Artemis, goddess of hunting, did not retaliate or defend her status as the greatest hunter, because she was enamored by Orion. This irritated Apollo, Artemis's twin, and he began to work with Gaia, the great earth goddess, to create a Scorpion that would kill Orion. Eventually, the pair battled, and the Scorpion won. Zeus then placed this creature in the sky in recognition of her good deed. The Scorpion was placed on the opposite end of the sky as Orion, to prevent them from fighting. It is said that Orion appears in the winter to hunt, fleeing in the summer when Scorpio appears. As a constellation, the fierceness and bravery of the Scorpion are immortalized, reminding us of her power—along with the fate of Orion's hubris and brutality.

SAGITTARIUS

THE PHILOSOPHER

November 22–December 21

RULING PLANET	Jupiter, Planet of Luck and Expansion
SYMBOL	The Centaur
MAIN DESCRIPTORS	Inspiring / Restless
DUALITY	Masculine
ELEMENT	Fire
QUALITY	Mutable
KEYWORD	I PERCEIVE
BODY PARTS	Hips and Thighs
COLOR	Orange, Color of Fiery Inspiration
CRYSTALS	Amethyst, Garnet, Smoky Quartz
ATTRIBUTES	Adventurous, Big-Minded, Honest, Reckless, Frank
INTERESTS	Traveling, Horseback Riding, Camping, Exploring, Archery
DRIVE	To Seek Truth

PROGRESSION AND PLANET

Sagittarius continues Scorpio's quest for wisdom, moving his focus from deep inner work up to the horizon, where he joyfully seeks truth and adventure. Opposite Gemini, whose quest is to gather knowledge, Sagittarius's path is to transform that knowledge into wisdom, sometimes by pursuing higher education. Ruled by Jupiter, planet of religion and exaggeration, Sagittarius readily forms beliefs and philosophies, sometimes taking them too far. This could manifest as dogma or recklessness, as Sagittarius asserts his conclusions with vigor and force. At the same time, Sagittarius possesses tremendous optimism, cheerfulness, and humor. He is unbound by limitation, just like Jupiter, his mighty ruler. A fiery and zealous thrill seeker, Sagittarius often becomes an athlete or avid outdoorsman.

SYMBOL

Symbolized by the Centaur and Archer, Sagittarius points his arrow toward abstract truth and faraway lands, galloping into the distance to gather experiences and wisdom. Half horse, half man, the Centaur has animal strength and stamina, along with the human ability to philosophize. A straight shooter, no sign has more candor, which can be both a gift and a curse. Sagittarius speaks his mind, sometimes pushing his own beliefs onto others. Keeping his ideologies in check, no sign is more inspiring, helping others to broaden their horizons by introducing them to expansive views and experiences.

The Greek myth of Sagittarius is connected to the archer Chiron, who was a gentle and compassionate centaur. While many centaurs lacked intelligence and acted out in violence, Chiron was known for his wisdom and ability to teach. One day, while trying to wipe out other centaurs who were causing problems, Heracles shot Chiron by accident. Finding Chiron suffering and helpless from his venomous arrows, Heracles experienced deep regret and sadness. Chiron was immortal and could not die—although he wanted to, since he was in so much pain. Prometheus stepped in after observing Chiron's struggles, and helped elevate him to the heavens, where he would live as the constellation Sagittarius. There, he reminds us of his wisdom, teaching, and gentle might.

♑

CAPRICORN

THE BUSINESSMAN

December 22–January 19

RULING PLANET	Saturn, Planet of Responsibility and Structure
SYMBOL	The Goat
MAIN DESCRIPTORS	Diligent / Repressive
DUALITY	Feminine
ELEMENT	Earth
QUALITY	Cardinal
KEYWORD	I USE
BODY PARTS	Knees and Bones
COLOR	Brown, Color of Wood, Nature, and Tradition
CRYSTALS	Tiger's Eye, Peridot, Jet
ATTRIBUTES	Driven, Persevering, Distinguished, Restrained, Disciplined, Traditional
INTERESTS	Playing Music, Collecting Antiques, Comedy, Gardening, Rock Climbing
DRIVE	To Accomplish

PROGRESSION AND PLANET

Moving from Sagittarius, who orients toward adventure and philosophy, we continue the zodiacal journey into Capricorn's firm dedication to society, family, tradition, and accomplishment. How can we create efficient systems? This is a key question for Capricorn. Ruled by Saturn, planet of restriction, time, and traditions, Capricorn possesses tremendous discipline. She is able to achieve whatever she wants, through ambition and perseverance. While she tends to mask her true feelings for the sake of propriety, Capricorn also has a way of loosening up and becoming more youthful with age. The sign of the father and the wise elder, Capricorn is traditional, sometimes strict, possessing ample integrity. Whether thinking about society, business endeavors, or family, she is always attuned to how she can create networks that are functional and supportive. Honest, humorous, and often musically inclined, Capricorn's steadiness and sense of timing can be her biggest assets.

SYMBOL

Symbolized by the Sea-Goat, Capricorn has two sides—the mountain goat and the fish. She can climb the mountains of success and social prestige, while also diving deep into the ocean of wisdom. Harnessing practicality, she places one foot in front of the other, moving steadily, with a strong sense of purpose and intention. Practical and restrained, she prioritizes achieving the task at hand, sometimes at any cost. Dedicated to reaching the highest peaks in all of her endeavors, the Goat does not lose sight of the ideals gleaned from Sagittarius. She applies determination to creating strong family units, as well as the systems and structures that form the basis of society. A mature

Capricorn is more inclined to use her fishtail, diving deep into the wells of emotion before laying a foundation or beginning her steady rise to accomplishment.

MYTH

The Greek myth connected with Capricorn is the story of the sea-goat Pricus. He was the father of a whole race of sea-goats who had the heads and bodies of goats and the tails of fish. They lived in the sea, close to shore, and were known as honorable and intelligent creatures. Created by Chronos, god of time, Pricus shared Chronos's ability to manipulate time. As the story goes, Pricus's children began exploring and swimming to shore. On land, they slowly lost their tails, intelligence, and ability to speak and live in the sea. Pricus was distraught. His children were disappearing from the water, rapidly becoming regular goats. To fix this, he reversed time and warned the sea-goats of their fate in attempts to save them. No matter how many times he did this, Pricus's children continued to leave the sea to explore. Finally, he gave up, allowing them to live out their karma. Immortal and in pain, he begged Chronos to help him die. Instead, Chronos placed him in the sky, where he could watch his children from above, even as they played on the highest peaks. There, Capricorn reminds us of paternal love, the inevitability of karma, and the importance of letting go.

AQUARIUS

THE INVENTOR

RULING PLANETS	Saturn and Uranus, Planets of Responsibility and Freedom
SYMBOL	The Water Bearer
MAIN DESCRIPTORS	Original / Shocking
DUALITY	Masculine
ELEMENT	Air
QUALITY	Fixed
KEYWORD	I KNOW
BODY PART	Ankles
COLOR	Violet, the Color of Insight and the Future
CRYSTALS	Amethyst, Garnet
ATTRIBUTES	Original, Eccentric, Futuristic, Shocking, Humanitarian
INTERESTS	Inventing, Humanitarianism, Sci-Fi, Community Organizing, Technology
DRIVE	To Be Free

PROGRESSION AND PLANET

Aquarius progresses from Capricorn's traditionalism to qualities of inventiveness, future orientation, and rebellion against the status quo. Without the energy of Aquarius, society would not progress. Feeding off shock, Aquarius loves to present us with the unexpected. Ideas flash into his mind like lightning, seemingly from the future. Ruled by Saturn and Uranus, planets of social responsibility and revolution, Aquarius applies his creative genius to furthering humanity. Somewhat cool and aloof, Aquarius is often more comfortable loving humanity at large than being in intimate, personal relationships. His tendency toward surprise can fall into needless disruption, trauma, and the creation of chaos—in which Aquarius thrives. However, the combination of system-loving Saturn and humanitarian Uranus make for an evolved Aquarius, skilled at creating inspired communities. He brings people together with shared purpose, brightening society while fostering tolerance and personal liberation. He has the intelligence and foresight to understand that true freedom is only real with organization and discipline. Ruling electricity, technology, and sudden breakthroughs, Aquarius often facilitates scientific innovation or spiritual revelation.

SYMBOL

Symbolized by the Water Bearer, Aquarius is one of the signs represented as a human-being, along with Virgo the Virgin and Gemini the Twins. The Water Bearer offers water—the sustenance of life and spirituality—and he does so without sacrificing his individuality or independence. Water washes away the past and clears the way for a future more connected with purity and enlightenment. A visionary, the Water Bearer carries a vessel that symbolizes open-ended spirituality—available to all in equal measure. Water itself represents the collective unconscious, along with the sea of interconnection. As the second to last sign, Aquarius is preparing us for Pisces, the last stop of the zodiac, which represents transcendence. In this way, Aquarius the Water Bearer is the height of human possibility before dissolving into spirituality, nonconceptuality, and oneness.

MYTH

The Greek myth associated with Aquarius is the story of Ganymede, a young prince who was said to be the most beautiful man of Troy. One day, tending to his father's sheep, Ganymede was spotted by Zeus, who found him to be overwhelmingly desirable. Zeus decided he wanted to take Ganymede as his servant and young lover—a common practice in ancient Greece. Once on Mount Olympus, Ganymede became Zeus's cupbearer, bringing Zeus drinks upon command. Essentially, Ganymede was Zeus's slave, and Zeus cemented this role by paying Ganymede's father with land and a herd of fine horses. One day Ganymede rebelled, pouring out all of Zeus's wine, ambrosia, and water of the gods onto Earth, which caused a massive flood. After reflection, Zeus realized he had been unkind to Ganymede and decided to make him immortal rather than punish him. Zeus then placed him in the stars as the constellation Aquarius. There, the Water Bearer reminds us of rebellion and independence—and the chaos sometimes necessary when fighting for freedom and equality.

♓

PISCES

THE DREAMER

February 19–March 20

RULING PLANET	Neptune, Planet of Spirituality
SYMBOL	The Fish
MAIN DESCRIPTORS	Imaginative / Spacey
DUALITY	Feminine
ELEMENT	Water
QUALITY	Mutable
KEYWORD	I BELIEVE
BODY PART	Feet
COLOR	Turquoise, the Color of the Ocean and Depth
CRYSTALS	Aquamarine, Fluorite, Lapis Lazuli
ATTRIBUTES	Dreamy, Mystical, Impressionable, Tender, Passive, Poetic
INTERESTS	Photography and Film, Meditation, Spirituality, Painting, Partying
DRIVE	To Embody Unconditional Love

PROGRESSION AND PLANET

As the final stop on the zodiacal journey, Pisces embodies all that came before her—the ultimate shift into oneness. Ruled by Neptune—planet of dreams, spirituality, and illusion—Pisces loves to escape into her inner world, playing in imaginative and otherworldly realms. As such, she can sometimes seem spacey and disconnected. The most spiritual and mystical sign, Pisces dissolves walls between the material and invisible realms, and between self and other. Having journeyed through all the other signs, she has empathy for everyone, understanding people and meeting them where they are. Impressionable and sensitive, she can merge with others' energies, and must be wary of who she keeps close. However, her ability to see into people's hearts is unparalleled. She has tremendous capacity to generate spiritual art and unconditional love, which she shares with the world—helping the rest of us reach her natural state of transcendence.

SYMBOL

Pisces is symbolized by two Fish who swim in opposite directions. The word *Pisces* means "fish" in Latin. Feeling pulled by the duality of being human, Pisces struggles to be both spiritual and human, tied to the material realm while floating in space. It is also said that one Fish is swimming upstream toward transcendence, while the other brings that wisdom downstream, back into the world. The two Fish embody receptivity, as Pisces possesses the capacity to understand opposing views and all facets of human nature and existence. Swimming effortlessly through any current, the Fish can blend with their surroundings, accommodating all that arises. Pisces is therefore the most compassionate of signs, embodying universal love, totality, forgiveness, and understanding.

MYTH

According to Greek myth, Pisces is connected to Aphrodite (goddess of beauty) and her son Eros (god of love). One day, the monster Typhoon began to appear on Mount Olympus, sent by Gaia to attack the gods. None of the gods had the power to destroy Typhoon, so they transformed themselves into animals to flee from him. On a certain day, when Typhoon appeared, Pan warned the others and then transformed himself into a sea-goat, diving into the Euphrates River. Aphrodite and Eros were bathing on the banks of the river and missed Pan's warning. When Typhoon suddenly appeared in the water, they turned themselves into Fish and swam away. Afterward, two Fish were placed in the sky as the Pisces constellation, commemorating the day when love and beauty were saved. Venus is the Roman name for Aphrodite, and astrologers consider Pisces to be Venus exalted—or exalted love—and to represent the spiritual dimensions of the Venusian realms of love and art.

2

THE SUN

Our Expression, Sanity, and Joy

THE SUN is our basic personality, identity, ego, and consciousness. Our primary sign, it is the most powerful indicator of who we are. The other planets, or aspects of our psyche, revolve around the Sun. It is the central archetype of our identity.

No matter the weather, the Sun is always there. Obvious and bright, or shrouded in clouds, our basic being is constantly shining. The journey connected to the Sun is discovering how we can grow into our unobstructed, fullest expression. Our Sun indicates how we can best feed our spirit, and also, how we are prone to unhealthy patterns. Similarly, it reveals how we can restore balance once we've fallen off-kilter.

For example, the life path for Sun in Virgo is about the pursuit of purity and moving toward spiritual perfection. Feeding her spirit would mean entering a role of service or devoting herself to a spiritual path. If she is out of balance, she may find that her quest for purity has turned into nitpicky perfectionism and judgment, both toward herself and others. Calibrating a Virgo's soul would require developing tremendous self-love, which she could then extend to others.

Embarking consciously on the journey of our Sun, exploring the neurotic and enlightened potentials of our energies, we can develop greater sanity and self-awareness, ruling our world from a place of conscious wisdom. The Sun gives us life, and we will feel our vitality depleted if we do not engage it. Since the Sun is our life force, self-worth, identity, and focus, if we aren't actively feeding it, we will feel weakened, cowardly, or even insane.

At its best, the Sun is our radiance and loving self-expression. At its worst, it becomes our arrogance or vanity. Bringing attention to our Sun's journey helps us shine our brightest so we can lead the fullest life possible.

The following chapter includes the journeys, gifts, and struggles of each Sun sign.

SUN IN ARIES
WARRIORSHIP

Fearlessness is not only possible, it is the ultimate joy.
When you touch nonfear, you are free.
—THICH NHAT HANH

ARIES ARCHETYPES

ENLIGHTENED **The Trailblazer, The Hero**
NEUROTIC **The Fighter, The Child**

ARIES JOURNEY:
BECOMING THE SELFLESS LEADER

Aries is the first sign of the zodiac. Represented by the Ram, Aries dives headlong into any project he initiates, fearlessly removing all obstacles in his way. In Tarot, Aries is the Fool. His courage is the result of innocence, or lack of experience. No memories of defeat can dampen his certainty. The journey of Sun in Aries is one of blending his self-confidence with patience and altruism. The Arian's spiritual growth comes from recognizing that he creates karma with each action he takes. He must develop restraint and consideration of others in order to master his warriorship. Then the Arian's true confidence will arise—from stillness and strength, rather than mindless action. He can extend his directness, bravery, and drive beyond selfish pursuits, harnessing them for the benefit of all.

ARIES GIFTS

KEYWORDS *initiative, decisiveness, willfulness, straightforwardness, leadership*

Aries is a true leader. No other sign can make a decision with such ease or confidence. Fiery and passionate, Aries possesses the gift of initiative. We can understand him better by considering Libra, his opposite. Libra is often stuck in indecision, carefully considering both sides of every situation to the point of stagnation. This is not a problem for the Arian, who is able to think on his feet, springing into action, and directing others according to his whims of inspiration. Because of this, some of the most successful entrepreneurs and executives have Sun in Aries.

Arians are straightforward and honest. What you see is who they really are, and what they say is what they really mean. If Arians change their mind, they will have no problem expressing it or immediately correcting course. With incredible will and focus, they have the ability to make things happen, leading the way with bold ideas and limitless drive.

Qualities of curiosity and courage, along with their desire to lead, help Aries to inspire whoever is around. Enterprising and convincing, he encourages others to follow him on any path he chooses to blaze.

With childlike naiveté, the Ram can find his own way, exploring and discovering his surroundings with freshness and enthusiasm. He is a renegade who can accomplish much good—as long as he takes the time to begin from pure intention, and to develop thoughtfulness and restraint. If he does, Aries' direct, uncomplicated nature becomes his biggest asset.

ARIES STRUGGLES

KEYWORDS *selfishness, brashness, impatience, impulsivity, intolerance*

When out of balance, Aries can become dominant, confrontational, self-absorbed, or insensitive. Their fierce independence makes it difficult to compromise in relationships. Lacking self-restraint, Arians can be temperamental at times, blowing up childishly, or being careless and unkind.

While Arians possess their own brand of charm—straightforward and self-assured—others can feel bulldozed by their force of opinions and lack of tact. Key lessons for Aries are to slow down and bring projects and ideas to completion. They must learn to stop and listen to opposing points of view, developing composure, tolerance, and balance in their daily lives.

If Arians can harness their vast stores of vitality and direct them toward the greater good, their trailblazing could spark fires of inspiration while initiating much-needed change in the world. By developing receptivity and self-restraint, Arians can become fearless warriors, leading the rest of us out of both danger and stagnation.

SUN IN TAURUS
SENSUALITY

When the distraction of the tongue is removed, the heart listens.
—THEODORE DREISER

TAURUS ARCHETYPES

ENLIGHTENED The Artisan, The Sensualist
NEUROTIC The Narcissist, The Materialist

TAURUS JOURNEY:
DEVELOPING HEALTHY SELF-WORTH

Ruled by Venus, planet of love and beauty, Taurus is slow and sensual, connected to the arts related to the earth and touch. The sense pleasures are everything to Taurus, who can deeply appreciate the sounds of bassy cello, the softness of cashmere, the flavors of rustic food, or the smell of a garden after it rains. Taureans are here to provide the rest of us ground and practicality. They remind us of silence, and our connection to the earth and our bodies. The journey of Taurus is to develop a healthy sense of self-worth and to surrender their strong attachment to material security, wealth, and vanity. Then, the evolved Taurus can help others to heal, awakening us through their touch and the embodiment of worthiness and strength.

TAURUS GIFTS

KEYWORDS *stillness, beauty, groundedness, generosity, compassion*

Taureans have many gifts, particularly in the realms of creativity and the tactile arts—such as cooking, ceramics, and woodworking. Sensual lovers, they take their time to explore another's body, relishing sensations with intention and purpose. Averse to drama, Taureans are difficult to fight with. Staying firm in their heart centers, they seldom allow their thoughts to spin into aggravation. This would unroot the Taurean, which she rarely permits.

Taureans easily magnetize people, providing ground for groundless souls. They're mesmerizing in the ways they move and dance, in the food they cook, the scents they wear, and their careful adornments. Since physical space is important to Taurus, beauty abounds in their homes. Often builders, they have a knack for buying and building furniture and for choosing pleasurable and earthy fabrics and decorations.

The Bull emits an effortless but powerful energy, remaining close to the earth with reassuring dependability. Her kindness and steadfastness are healing for many, as she reminds us of the power of silence, and the profundity that comes when we stop speaking and open fully to our senses.

TAURUS STRUGGLES

KEYWORDS *self-doubt, rigidity, overindulgence, materialism, vanity*

Sometimes Taurus's commitment to the earth falls off-kilter. She becomes too rigid, protecting her heart, fearing that if she softens, she will fall apart or lose control. The key for Taurus is to develop a strong sense of worthiness. After all, she rules self-worth. Somehow, she has to face her shadows and love herself fully. Surrender is important for

Taurus. Not only must she yield to her shadows, she must also release her unhealthy attachments and indulgences. From there, she can allow her steady and generous compassion to shine through.

If Taurus is able to let go of rigidity and possessiveness, she will be able to attract whatever she wants. Diving into her natural ability to love wholeheartedly, she can open to a deeper sense of intimacy and self-acceptance. Taurus is an earth god or goddess, planting us in the ground so we may root down and grow up, reaching to the sky of wisdom and oneness.

As the Taurean shows us the earth's beauty, she must remember to relax her fixation on physical appearance, as well as an exaggerated desire for material wealth and security. Real abundance comes from generosity and extending her love and acceptance to all beings. Growing into her true self, Taureans realize that they have all that they need within themselves—including deep contentment and a strong connection to ordinary magic. They will be able to heal others with the power of their touch, while offering a beautiful container of groundedness and security.

SUN IN GEMINI
INTELLIGENCE

All important words, all the words marked for grandeur by
a poet, are keys to the universe, to the dual universe of the
Cosmos and the depths of the human spirit.
—GASTON BACHELARD

GEMINI ARCHETYPES

ENLIGHTENED **The Teacher, The Expert**
NEUROTIC **The Dictator, The Phony**

GEMINI JOURNEY:
JOINING INTELLECT WITH HEART

Gemini rules intellect, and no other sign is more witty, sociable, or adept at teaching and communication. The Twins are the most human sign of the zodiac, and represent the duality of earthly existence—both the physical person and the spirit. Geminis play with this seeming contradiction, often forgetting that we don't have to ping-pong between them; we embody both. As Gemini moves through life, he must learn to drop into his heart, merging his intellectual mind with the emotional body. In this way, Gemini's journey is to deepen his knowledge and use it as a pathway to wisdom. Possessing tremendous mental energy, he must also find a way to settle his thoughts. From there, he can open his heart to spirituality and universal love.

GEMINI GIFTS

KEYWORDS *intelligence, wit, clarity, curiosity, liveliness*

Articulate and highly intelligent, Geminis are bright and engaging conversationalists. They explore all facets of ideas and situations, presenting informed points of view with sparkle and zeal. The Twins are masters of witty banter and debate. With clear minds and sharp tongues, they easily win arguments and sway others to their points of view.

Dinner parties would be dreary without the lively chatter of a Gemini. They have a knack for conversation—both listening and speaking. They can pull information from their vast stores of knowledge and offer it at the most compelling moments, impressing others with their nimble minds and ability to entertain.

Excellent writers, orators, journalists, and artists, they are very much committed to observing all things human, and they love to share this fascination with others. They inspire the rest of us to open to different perspectives and experiences, expanding our networks and frames of mind with agility and grace. Geminis live fully, making many friends throughout their lives, engaging in spirited exchanges, and exploring all facets of humanity and the world, with adaptability and ease. Their curiosity is perhaps their greatest asset, and they find mentors wherever they go. They ask astute questions in order expand their knowledge and vast stores of information, which to them is the ultimate prize.

GEMINI STRUGGLES

KEYWORDS *restlessness, unreliability, manipulation, nervousness, duplicity*

Intellect without heart is dangerous. As Geminis' energies swirl primarily around their heads, they sometimes struggle to drop into their hearts. If a Gemini is out of balance, he can poison the well, propagating ideas that are morally corrupt or harmful, both to himself and others. The key for Gemini is to meditate, allowing the snow globe of his brilliant, active mind to settle to the ground. From here, he can connect with his body and heart, then make more genuine decisions.

Geminis may find commitment difficult, as they're easily bored and intrigued by a variety of experiences. They need constant stimulation as well as stimulating friends. If Gemini could direct his interest more fully to one person, he might find that each individual is endlessly fascinating, that we all have beautiful mythological tapestries within us, filled with limitless wisdom.

Herein lies the key to resolving Gemini's struggles. His inquisitive and quick mind can provide a beautiful path to wisdom, as long as he grounds his knowledge in ultimate truth and a bigger picture of morality, emotional investments, and purpose. It would benefit Gemini to study with an open heart and tears in his eyes, remembering to integrate both sides of himself—the intellect and the heart. As his path to wisdom unfolds, Gemini can become an excellent teacher, as long as he points people to their own experience, rather than imposing his points of view.

SUN IN CANCER
SENSITIVITY

Real fearlessness is the product of tenderness. It comes from
letting the world tickle your heart, your raw and beautiful heart.
You are willing to open up, without resistance or shyness, and face the
world. You are willing to share your heart with others.

—CHÖGYAM TRUNGPA RINPOCHE

CANCER ARCHETYPES

ENLIGHTENED The Nurturer, The Sensitive
NEUROTIC The Moper, The Grouch

CANCER JOURNEY:
MASTERING EMOTIONAL SENSITIVITY

The most sensitive and emotional of all signs, Cancer the Crab is a feeler
and a psychic. When she enters a room, she can feel what everyone else
is feeling. Easily overwhelmed, she retreats into her shell, pulling out
her pincers and unleashing her powerful moods. The journey for Sun
in Cancer is to learn how to protect her sensitivity so she can use it as
a gift, extending her penetrating compassion to others as the nurturing
universal mother. Cancer must develop tremendous self-awareness.
Then, when her feelings consume her, she can recognize them and gently return to her center. As she masters this work, she accomplishes
important work for all of us—feeling the depths of human existence,
relinquishing barriers between ourselves and others, and demonstrating a continual return to love, acceptance, and trust.

CANCER GIFTS

KEYWORDS *gentleness, imagination, perceptiveness, supportiveness, hospitality*

Cancer is wonderfully imaginative and perceptive, frequently turning inward to her rich, magical world of daydream. She is a wonderful hostess who loves to invite friends to her house to nurture them in her favorite manner—cooking and caretaking. She creates a sense of hospitality and safety that envelops her guests like a warm bath. Afterward, they return to their own houses with beautiful lessons on how to create feelings of home and comfort, both physically and within themselves.

Cancerians can dive into your emotions, feel them with you, and cuddle and love you, no matter your state of mind. They can softly mirror your own depth, while melting into your being. In this way, Cancers are devotional. They love their friends and family deeply and naturally, extending maternal kindness and support without hesitation.

Possessing inherent strength, Cancer often demonstrates a quality of toughness, which manifests as a shell that protects her vulnerability. She can accomplish much in the world by allowing her intuition, heart, and apt perception to guide her. This is Cancer at her best—guard down, surrendering herself to gravity and chance, fearlessly exposing her eternal love for all humans.

CANCER STRUGGLES

KEYWORDS *moodiness, vulnerability, suspicion, smothering, insecurity*

To be a balanced Cancer, the Crab must be willing to come out of her shell, release the security of her tough exterior, and reveal her soft and nurturing essence. She must learn to feel the cruelty of the human heart while remaining open—loving all aspects of humanity, beginning with herself. Otherwise, a triggered Cancer can be moody, sharp, and indirect.

If Cancer does not feel safe, she can become hardened—even engaging in her own acts of cruelty because she has closed her heart, hiding behind her shell and pincers. If loving and supportive people are not surrounding her, she could take on the savagery of others, losing the courage to be vulnerable.

It is vital for Cancer to master human emotion, both her own and others. She must learn how to psychically protect herself so she can walk into the world with her innate sensitivity, while remaining kind and genuine. If she does, she becomes the world's mother, ever-compassionate, loving, and forgiving of all human atrocities. She can understand people like no other, seeing to their core with X-ray vision. If she chooses to reveal herself, rather than hiding behind her masks, she can become the ultimate symbol of universal love and compassion. This is Cancer's true nature.

SUN IN LEO

HEART

Radiate boundless love toward the entire world—above, below, and across—unhindered, without ill will, without enmity.
—BUDDHA

LEO ARCHETYPES

ENLIGHTENED The Performer, The Loving King
NEUROTIC The Show-Off, The Autocrat

LEO JOURNEY:
EXPANDING INTO UNCONDITIONAL LOVE

Leo is the most regal and creative Sun sign. Represented by the Lion and ruled by the Sun itself, Leo beams light from his enormous heart. Fiercely loyal, Leos can become too fixed on the objects of their affection. To grow into the King or Queen of Hearts, which is their true purpose, Leos must raise their gaze from personal love to limitless compassion. They must rule from their hearts, unobstructed by ego and selfish pursuits—fearlessly expanding their immense love to include all beings. As always this must begin by truly loving themselves, not with ego, but with genuine embrace.

LEO GIFTS

KEYWORDS *creativity, playfulness, humor, affection, self-expression*

Leo is highly playful and affectionate. The planet of ego in the sign of personality means that Leo is able to fully express himself, with exuberance, creativity, and humor. In the company of a Leo, we could feel like the Moon—illuminated, receiving and reflecting back their bright light.

Leo wants nothing more than to entertain and perform for whoever is around. The Lion brings smiles to receptive audiences, while offering courage and inspiration to shyer personalities. When pursuing creative outlets, Leo shines brightest, relishing in laughter, while connecting people with their hearts—fully, simply, and directly.

Natural leaders, Leos can inspire us to remember joy, no matter the task. Held in the radiance of their open hearts, they reveal that we can accomplish anything with delight. Without enjoyment, what's the point? Leo has a childlike innocence that will win us over and lead us in good times, until we smile so big our cheeks hurt. Cuddlers and jokers, they melt us with their devotion and warm affection.

LEO STRUGGLES

KEYWORDS *boastfulness, codependence, exaggeration, arrogance, self-absorption*

When out of balance, Leo's natural courage can become prideful and arrogant. Without an audience, he feels incomplete and unworthy, exaggerating his talents with showiness out of desperation to feel lovable. Part of Leos' work is to recognize that their light radiates whether or not someone is there to receive it. In searching for others to reflect their love, they may have forgotten that love transcends giver and receiver—one of their most important lessons.

Others may feel angered by Leo as the Lion's longing for appreciation and admiration can come across as self-absorption, vanity, hunger for power, or conceit. To become the loving king or queen, Leo must remember to surrender personal desire, and that we are ultimately working for the benefit of all. Then he can move closer to his enlightened state—recognizing his faults and gifts with honesty, expressing creativity with humor, loving himself fully, and extending that love to all.

Sad Leos are ones who have forgotten the joy of generosity, who have started to believe they are unworthy of pleasure, or who have become too fixated on one person or ego pursuits. An awakened Leo is a selfless, radiant leader, who inspires others to live from their hearts, and to express themselves fearlessly. When Leo demonstrates this, life becomes effortless, for the Lion is embodying his genuine nature.

SUN IN VIRGO
PURITY

We don't set out to save the world; we set out to wonder how other people
are doing and to reflect on how our actions affect other people's hearts.

—PEMA CHÖDRÖN

VIRGO ARCHETYPES

ENLIGHTENED The Angel, The Devotee
NEUROTIC The Worrier, The Judge

VIRGO JOURNEY:
ATTAINING SPIRITUAL PERFECTION

Sun in Virgo brings emphasis to purity and devotion. The ultimate journey of Virgo is one of spiritual perfection, attained through her natural
humility. She surrenders ego readily through hard work and service to
others. More than any other Sun sign, Virgo is able to see the best in people, never giving up on anyone. The key for the Virgin is to love herself
fully, and to find balance in her perfectionism. Otherwise she'll use her
shortcomings as weapons against herself. As she relaxes and releases
judgment, Virgo can embrace her journey of spiritual awakening, gently examining her weaknesses with honesty and forgiveness. While
she connects easily with spirit and magic, Virgoans are also very much
creatures of this planet. Their awakened selves are much like angels,
connecting human beings with spirit, and bringing heaven to earth.

VIRGO GIFTS

KEYWORDS *loyalty, sensitivity, hard work, practicality, purity*

No friend is more loyal than sensitive, devoted Virgo, who works tirelessly to help whoever is in need. Unafraid of difficult emotions, she can see to the heart of a person or situation with logic and clarity, using her mental gifts and pragmatism to solve seemingly impossible problems. She is a lifelong friend who you can always trust will remember that no matter what, we are all basically good.

Caring deeply for animals and children, Virgo loves purity and retains her natural innocence no matter what. She is thoughtful, paying much attention to detail, surprising others with all that she notices. She will take the time to process conversations and relationships, and is one of the most likely signs to write genuine, well-constructed love letters. Ruled by Mercury, planet of communication, language is one of her gifts, and she will think carefully about her words before expressing her thoughts.

As you earn a Virgo's trust, you will unearth an affectionate, warm, and magical friend and lover, who will bless you with her deep and lasting love. The main requirement is that you respect your Virgo, never taking her for granted.

VIRGO STRUGGLES

KEYWORDS *worry, spinning, judgment, criticism, righteousness*

No one worries more than dear Virgo, who seems to have a hamster wheel living inside her head. Her careful mind can easily teeter into overanalysis, as she mulls over unimportant minutiae. In pursuit of spiritual perfection, the Virgoan can become self-critical, particularly if she hasn't developed proper self-love or the ability to forgive herself. This self-judgment can easily turn on those around her, as she looks down from her high horse, irritating others with her nitpicking and righteousness.

Virgo's real work is to look in the mirror with her clear and honest vision, and to embrace the totality of her being, loving herself fully. She must be able to recognize her strengths and weaknesses, with both humility and full appreciation. If she can commit to this work, she will be able to deepen her understanding of nuance and human complexity while also unlocking her extraordinary gifts. She can learn to shine her pure light onto others, helping them to heal and love themselves—just as she has done for herself.

As she stops her mind's spinning and embraces her whole self, she could even become an important person for the world's healing, creating environments of sanity, order, selflessness, and magic. The rest of us can look to Virgo as a pristine example of devotion, service to others, and tenacious dedication to purity and spiritual perfection.

SUN IN LIBRA
HARMONY

We are so lightly here. It is in love that
we are made. In love we disappear.
—LEONARD COHEN

LIBRA ARCHETYPES

ENLIGHTENED **The Artist, The Lover**
NEUROTIC **The Dilettante, The Liar**

LIBRA JOURNEY:
MASTERING PARADOX

Libra is the most romantic placement for the Sun. Represented by the Scales, Librans balance two opposing sides in order to reach perfect equilibrium. This is exactly the journey of Sun in Libra: to attain absolute inner harmony through the mastery of paradox. Who else can hold two conflicting truths, simultaneously and effortlessly? Right and wrong, good and bad, light and dark, the Libran understands that both sides are valid and true, and that enlightenment comes from approaching life with equanimity and an open heart.

LIBRA GIFTS

KEYWORDS *equilibrium, beautification, appreciation, charm, romance*

Librans are wonderfully charming friends—ones who don't judge our temporary insanity, who balance aggression with spaciousness and neutrality, and who help everyone they meet feel loved and appreciated. Librans' artistic and aesthetic talents come from their deep yearning for harmony. In a constant quest for equilibrium, Librans create phenomenal beauty along their path. Playing the perfect song, bringing home the most exquisite flowers, discovering the most beautiful hike or the most interesting wine to be enjoyed by friends, are all tactics for the Libran to relax and help others do the same.

Sometimes this means that Librans become talented artists, designers, or musicians. They create art with the intention of establishing their own peace, which is fragile, requiring effort to maintain. They refine their relationship to the arts, appreciating them fully. They are able to create paintings, spaces, or music that can help soothe our senses.

Librans can also be the greatest lovers, understanding the art of sweet nothings—expressing their romantic feelings, which come so easily to them. Their hearts can dance with their partners' as they instantly discover another's beauty, harmonizing their frequency in perfect pitch.

LIBRA STRUGGLES

KEYWORDS *dishonesty, indecision, dilettantism, people-pleasing, avoidance*

The problem is that Libra, in a commitment to maintaining his fragile inner peace, can end up merely skimming the surface, unwilling to delve into grit, sometimes telling half-truths to avoid confrontation. While Librans rule love and can be wonderful partners, they also struggle more than any other sign in this very domain. In fact, relationships are their main path to personal growth. Anxiety can arise as they sense the scales tipping out of balance, which so often happens in deep relationships. People pleasers, they may disappear to avoid confrontation, seeking love elsewhere without informing their partners. They do so to maintain love in their lives while avoiding hurt feelings.

Librans also have trouble agreeing with any strong opinion, feeling compelled to calmly present an opposing point of view—no matter their own. They teeter with their commitments and decision making, easily seeing the positives and negatives of every situation. How can someone so comfortable in paradox possibly take a stand or choose one option? How can someone who discovers beauty at every corner decide to stay on one corner for the rest of their life?

Dilettantism, struggles keeping promises, and dishonesty are all indications that Libra is out of whack and operating from neurosis. The key to restoring balance, the focus of their journey, is to dive fully into darkness and whatever they fear. They can find harmony in the depths—beauty in their sadness and richness in their anger—while opening their hearts to the uglier aspects of themselves and humanity. These are the signs of an awakened Libra.

SUN IN SCORPIO
TRANSFORMATION

And the day came when the risk to remain tight in a bud
was more painful than the risk it took to blossom. —ANAÏS NIN

SCORPIO ARCHETYPES

ENLIGHTENED The Shaman, The Alchemist
NEUROTIC The Repressor, The Destroyer

SCORPIO JOURNEY:
SURRENDERING CONTROL

Sun in Scorpio contains extraordinary power and depth. A Scorpion's journey is not one for the faint of heart. It requires full commitment to embracing our chaos and confusion, to exploring our deepest psyche and the full spectrum of human experience. If a Scorpio masters the art of transmutation—if she can welcome her explosions of emotion, which rise like lava—she will discover her underlying wisdom. She will be able to wear her pain as adornment, as it becomes an important step toward spiritual awakening. In this way, the Scorpion embodies both healing and destruction, death and rebirth. She must surrender to the full intensity of her emotions, throwing them to the fire and then rising from the ashes—wiser and more purified. The enlightened Scorpion helps those with severe affliction. Unafraid of intensity, she guides us through the painful hell realms that stem from our own minds. Scorpio can show us the path of fearless surrender. She teaches us, just as she's learned, to stay open and relinquish our control.

SCORPIO GIFTS

KEYWORDS *passion, bravery, depth, mysticism, transformation*

When we are at our lowest—a break in sanity, the death of a loved one, or rejection from a lover—there is no greater friend than Scorpio. She is able to stay with us through our darkest hours, keep our secrets, and cry with us wholeheartedly. Scorpios live in deep waters, and if you find yourself there, they will stay by your side, helping you swim. Excellent therapists, they are ever willing to explore the twisted shapes of the human heart, with fearlessness and intensity. They love to investigate—not only emotion, but also science, the tangible world, and how things come together and fall apart.

Passionate and sexual, mystical and mysterious, Scorpions can guide us to the places that we've always been curious about, but never had the courage to visit. They push our boundaries, helping us expand our points of view to include previously unfathomed feelings and experiences. By opening to the depths, Scorpio shows us that we can transform sadness into richness by revealing that it was richness all along. She enjoys and embraces the darker emotions and hidden dimensions of reality. We all have darkness, but Scorpio can't help but express these sides of herself, sometimes violently. She reflects back our shadows so we can face and integrate them, becoming more self-aware.

The enlightened Scorpion demonstrates that if we don't resist heartbreak, our hearts will grow bigger as we feel more connected with others. If we're willing to dip into the cauldron with an awakened Scorpion, anything is possible. She will lead us to our own enlightenment, healing us by teaching us to transmute our suffering. She shows us that there is no such thing as pain and pleasure, good and bad—as long as we say yes to all that arises.

SCORPIO STRUGGLES

KEYWORDS *repression, explosiveness, vengefulness, obsession, possessiveness*

Living with a dark well of emotion, a danger exists for the unbalanced Scorpion to fall into fear and repression. Unable to regulate the confusion and chaos within, Scorpio could resort to obsessive-compulsion, attempting to control her environment, both externally and within herself. She could become jealous and possessive, even wanting to destroy her partners if she can't own them completely. Eventually the fuse will blow for imbalanced Scorpio. She will explode, revealing a maelstrom of emotion that she's been hiding behind thick walls.

Moody, sulky—and potentially abusive and destructive—neurotic Scorpions are denying their true nature. Afraid of their demons, they can become lost in self-absorption, repression, or addiction. They punish those around them as they project their unexamined shadows onto others. Any pain or self-loathing that they don't acknowledge, they will despise in whoever is close. Conversely, the Scorpion could have positive shadows, overwhelmed by envy for those who are demonstrating her unrealized potentials.

The key for Scorpio's journey is to understand the tremendous power they hold. They have the ability, more than any other sign, to face intense psychic undercurrents, without drowning. If the Scorpion can rouse courage and face whatever arises, she will discover her own secret—the gifts of deep wisdom, healing, and profundity. As Scorpio relaxes with her afflictions, inviting them to meet her exactly as they are, they will vanish instantly. If she lets go, plunging into darkness, she will find that she is able to open to an equal amount of light. We need among us such women and men, innate shamans who face the world's underbelly, helping us heal with the magic of surrender.

SUN IN SAGITTARIUS
WISDOM

I think that what we're seeking is an experience of being
alive, so that our life experiences on the purely physical
plane will have resonances with our own innermost being and
reality, so that we actually feel the rapture of being alive.

—JOSEPH CAMPBELL

SAGITTARIUS ARCHETYPES

ENLIGHTENED The Philosopher, The Yogi
NEUROTIC The Extremist, The Restless Wanderer

SAGITTARIUS JOURNEY:
TURNING KNOWLEDGE INTO WISDOM

The journey of Sun in Sagittarius involves exploration into unknown
territories. Sagittarius is the centaur, pointing his bow and arrow
toward the horizon. He seeks adventure and aims to expand his understanding as far as possible. Perhaps he does so through physical activity
and athletics, or by exploring the wisdom of the body through yoga
or qigong. Perhaps he pursues higher education, immersing himself
in philosophical studies. Whatever his method, the highest possible
accomplishment in the Sagittarian journey is to discover wisdom and
above all, the meaning of life, which words could never capture. His
searching could expand his consciousness to unimaginable reaches, as
long as he never believes anything too strongly. The path of the Sagittarian is to keep seeking, deepening, and furthering his understanding,
while never falling into the trap of dogma.

SAGITTARIUS GIFTS

KEYWORDS *idealism, adventurousness, optimism, wisdom, athleticism*

Sagittarius is adventurous, philosophical, and often athletic. He longs to travel to faraway places, both literally and in his mind. Funny, cheerful, and hard to pin down, Sagittarius leads others in good times, imbuing them with optimism and free-spiritedness. He courageously delves into anything outside the comfort of ordinary reality, as he explores other cultures, lands, religions, and systems of belief. Open to new situations and people, he is excited to expand his mind and understanding.

Wisdom cannot be gleaned through books alone. No one knows this better than the Sagittarian, who realizes that facts do not compare to real-life experience. He dives wholeheartedly into studies, then applies them to real life—contextualizing whatever he learns into his experiences. While his opposite, Gemini, is focused on gathering knowledge and playing within intellectual constraints, Sagittarius is far more interested in expanding his mind. He will go to the furthest reaches of conceptual exploration, inquiring into deeper reasons for why we would study anything—and why we are here at all.

The enlightened Sagittarian never stops prodding. He understands that if he solidifies his points of view, or reaches stagnation in his life or thinking, he has missed the point; he must point his arrow forward and push on. The true Sagittarian is liberated from all constraints, expanding beyond his narrow human mind. He continuously gathers experiences and adventures that shake his perspective. Then all that remains is wisdom and truth—the ultimate Sagittarian attainment.

SAGITTARIUS STRUGGLES

KEYWORDS *impatience, fanaticism, restlessness,
abstraction, confrontation*

An imbalanced Sagittarian can fall into various traps because of his overenthusiasm. Exceedingly zealous and trusting, he could run into harmful situations, unable to draw upon healthy skepticism and discernment. Sagittarian problems could include diving too fast into relationships or marriage, following questionable religions or doctrines, or finding himself in peril in faraway places.

The Sagittarian would benefit from tempering his exuberance, appetite, and lust. Otherwise, he could have trouble staying in one place, or with one person. The constant seeking, which is helpful for gleaning wisdom, could easily become restlessness or impatience. His fervor could turn into fanaticism if he forgets that the path will lead to truth, but is not truth itself. Meditation and discipline would be a great support for Sagittarius. Bringing increased awareness to his body, heart, and other people—noticing if he's gone too far in thought or action—could help him to assuage his extremism, while avoiding hurting himself or others.

Even in making mistakes, Sagittarius is able to expand his mind and heart through varied experiences. His courage in diving headlong into adventure makes him a fascinating character—one who has much to teach and share later in life, in spite of frequent blunders. Quick to fall into the trap of faulty thinking or behavior, he's just as apt to let them go. He is ready to bound forward into his next avenue of thought and adventure, never looking back.

SUN IN CAPRICORN
DILIGENCE

Only when you can be extremely pliable and soft
can you be extremely hard and strong.
—ZEN PROVERB

CAPRICORN ARCHETYPES

ENLIGHTENED The Businessman, The Dignitary
NEUROTIC The Social Climber, The Authoritarian

CAPRICORN JOURNEY:
MERGING VULNERABILITY WITH AMBITION

The journey of Sun in Capricorn is about balancing ambition and leadership with their feelings and inner lives, so they can embark wholeheartedly on making positive contributions to their family and society. In their highest frequency, Capricorns embody integrity. They apply patience and persistence to learning how to soften, open up, and clear their inclinations toward power, control, and seeking adulation. Once they do, whatever they set out to accomplish will be of benefit to the greater good—their true calling. Enlightened Capricorns tap in to their wisdom and heart, then place one foot in front of the other, establishing solid roots before beginning any journey. As long as they develop self-respect and healthy relationships to their innermost self, Capricorns can become significant people, infusing their worlds with dignity, decency, and humor.

CAPRICORN GIFTS

KEYWORDS *ambition, integrity, dependability, discipline, responsibility*

Capricorn is determined to reach her goals, possessing tremendous patience and tenacity to do so. The most traditional sign, Capricorn is symbolized by the father, placing utmost value on family—creating strong family units, spending time with relatives, and nurturing familial bonds. Capricorn's carefulness, reliability, and honesty ensure that she earns others' respect. A natural leader with hardwired composure and decorum, Capricorns have the strong ability to succeed. They understand the importance of taking their time to accomplish tasks thoroughly, while mastering the art of networking and delegation.

Capricorns have unparalleled self-discipline. When struggles and difficulties arise, they do not give up. Willful and determined, they plow through obstacles, seldom exhibiting outward displays of emotion. Trustworthy and diplomatic, Capricorn children seem like wise elders. Hardly in need of discipline, the young Capricorn is remarkably composed. She becomes younger with age, softening her rigidity later in life while expressing her innate humor more freely.

Enlightened Capricorns are comfortable with solitude. Slow and intentional, they operate from a place of dignity. They are examples of the best aspects of society—well-mannered, put together, and reliable, while working hard on projects that benefit the public. As long as they relax their inner worlds and learn to ease up on themselves, they can become excellent leaders, displaying unparalleled discipline, earthiness, pragmatism, and good timing.

CAPRICORN STRUGGLES

KEYWORDS *materialism, social climbing, stubbornness, opportunism, control*

Capricorn can become so fixed on a goal that she loses sight of the bigger picture. Her natural leadership could become overly controlling and domineering, and her emphasis on society could morph into an unhealthy preoccupation with image and material pursuits. As she obsesses over wealth and her public persona, she could end up repressing her emotions and the messier aspects of her being.

The key for Capricorn is to make sure that the sturdy foundations she builds align with her highest ideals. She constructs everything with incredible tenacity and attention to detail, so she must be sure to start with proper intention—considering if what she is working on will contribute positively to society. If she's disconnected from integrity, the imbalanced Capricorn could recalibrate by protecting her solitude—perhaps wandering off alone to engage in Capricornian interests, like nature, music, history, or antiques. This gives Capricorn time to reflect so she will make decisions from a more genuine place. The inner life is very important for Capricorn, who must be certain that her outer life and well-crafted endeavors begin from a tender place. Otherwise success could feel hollow—existing merely as a badge of power, fame, and social prestige.

Workaholism and loneliness are potential pitfalls for Capricorns. They must learn to balance home life with social life, allowing their fluidity and emotional expression to come forth, while upholding their commitment to decorum and social graces. The antidote for Capricornian neuroses is learning to relax, conveying their true selves in their public personas, and aligning their vocation with their most heartfelt desires.

SUN IN AQUARIUS
AUTHENTICITY

The privilege of a lifetime is to become who you truly are.
—C. G. JUNG

AQUARIUS ARCHETYPES

ENLIGHTENED **The Genius, The Humanitarian**
NEUROTIC **The Contrarian, The Robot**

AQUARIUS JOURNEY:
EXPERIENCING ULTIMATE FREEDOM

The journey of Sun in Aquarius has to do with discovering freedom—beginning with the mind, continuing with self-expression, and ending with community and humankind. Aquarians want to push boundaries and limits, destroying oppression with force as sudden as a lightning bolt. Renegades, Aquarians are important people because they progress humanity. They think outside the box and apply their ingenuity to discovering inventive solutions to problems of all kinds. The key for the Aquarian is to learn that true liberation begins within ourselves, that love for mankind is not a concept or thought, but a wholehearted feeling and experience. Once Aquarians learn to connect with their more personal heart and offer it to others, they will find ultimate freedom. From there, they can extend their hearts and gifts outward to their communities and culture at large.

AQUARIUS GIFTS

KEYWORDS *freedom, originality, inventiveness, progressiveness,*
humanitarianism

Aquarians are the most fascinating people to spend time with. Their minds dance through the ether, carrying us to unexpected terrains. When an Aquarian examines an object, philosophy, theory, or person, he sees them differently from the rest of us. He taps in to other dimensions, exposing interesting angles, which would have otherwise remained obscured. He solves problems quickly, finding inventive solutions with a single flash of his brilliant and original mind.

Creative geniuses, Aquarians are able to channel incredible insight. Their ideas are immense and seemingly impossible. But if you take the Water Bearer seriously and find pragmatic support for his unfathomable schemes, you will discover pathways to undiscovered terrain. They open our world into higher frequencies of thought and progression, which we could have never even imagined.

Aquarians are connectors. They bring people together in community, pointing out what makes each of us unique and waving their wands to clear obstacles in the way of our fullest expression. They shock us and make us laugh, saying the most unexpected things—unconstrained by propriety and supposed-tos. If you are able to set an Aquarian free, appreciating him with no expectations, you will have a most inspiring friend. He will show you the pathway to authenticity and original thought as he continuously displays his own.

AQUARIUS STRUGGLES

KEYWORDS *aloofness, unpredictability, stubbornness, contrarianism, perversion*

When out of balance, the Aquarian's lightning bolts could morph from enlightened activity and changing humanity for the better, to straight-up destruction with no purpose. When their hearts close, their healthy rebellion can become contentious as they act out against any energies they find oppressive. Frequently, Aquarians trigger people as they test waters and push envelopes, saying outrageous things. While this type of behavior can be helpful, pushing the limits of our comfort zones and egos, Aquarians can easily go too far, making enemies and hurting people unnecessarily.

Aquarians' focus on humanity can sometimes harm their personal relationships, as it's easier for them to love the concept of people than the actual gritty human being standing before them. They can become aloof and cold, finding it challenging to stay committed to the confines of their human bodies. The freedom to travel into conceptual and spiritual realms feels far more exciting, rewarding, and limitless.

The key for Aquarius is to find a way to love every human being the way he loves humanity, to remember that he is passionate about applying his insight and brilliance to the progression of humankind because each of us is a precious being. We are in this together as a group of individuals, reflecting love collectively and on our own. The enlightened Aquarian dives into intimacy, which helps to ground him. After all, we are human beings, and our true spiritual path begins with embracing this fully.

SUN IN PISCES
TRANSCENDENCE

To understand everything is to forgive everything.
—SIDDHARTHA GAUTAMA

PISCES ARCHETYPES

ENLIGHTENED The Spiritualist, The Dreamer
NEUROTIC The Martyr, The Escapist

PISCES JOURNEY:
BLENDING HEAVEN AND EARTH

The journey of Sun in Pisces is all-encompassing. In some ways, it represents the ultimate path of human awakening. The Piscean must learn to keep her feet planted firmly on earth, to take care of herself so she remains grounded while dissolving boundaries between the material and spiritual realms. She realizes that this life is all a dream, and she brings that understanding back to earth, back to being human. Then Pisceans can inspire others with their embodiment of this wisdom, which is unconditional love. They demonstrate—in their gentleness, otherworldly faces, and immense potential for forgiveness—that unconditional love is available to all of us. In fact, it's all there is.

PISCES GIFTS

KEYWORDS *forgiveness, spirituality, adaptability, gentleness, compassion*

Pisces can feel what everyone else feels, imbuing us with godlike empathy, limitless compassion, and a saintly ability to forgive, no matter how terrible the deed. She can walk into any space and adapt, shifting like water to surround any twists and shapes that appear, helping the room to feel full, supported, and complete. A welcome addition to parties, she goes with the flow, dissolving social tensions.

When she dances, she becomes the music; when she loves, her heart merges fully with her friends and partners. She has the uncanny ability to make others feel seen, understood, and appreciated. The Piscean also has the ability to dissolve walls, to melt away fears and inhibitions, opening others to true love and vulnerability.

Her ultimate gift is her spirituality. She easily channels spirit through artistic expression and journeys into other realms. If she learns to master groundedness and self-care, she can become an adept meditator and spiritualist, expertly showing others, without words or concepts, how they can tap in to their own higher minds. Pisceans can even be psychic, as they blur the boundaries that delineate space and time. They easily access the singular consciousness that connects us all.

PISCES STRUGGLES

KEYWORDS *escapism, victimization, inferiority, unworthiness, self-indulgence*

If Pisces forgets to set boundaries and take care of herself, she can easily fall into problems. Because she is empathetic and forgiving, she is more apt than other signs to attract abusive partners, less able to walk away from toxicity than more courageous, logical, or earthier signs. Because she is so fluid, and because she finds the separation between self and other to be so nebulous, she often forgets to connect with the strength of her dignity—which has nothing to do with other people's perceptions.

One of the keys to creating more harmony in a Piscean soul is to develop a strong sense of worthiness—the understanding that she is okay exactly the way that she is, regardless of external validation. If Pisces can realize that she has dominion over herself and her circumstances, if she can trust herself to set boundaries when other people mistreat her, she can let go of her tendency toward martyrdom. She can grow into the understanding that by allowing bad behavior, she ultimately betrays herself. This means she has more power than she sometimes likes to admit, but by owning this power, she becomes more of who she is—embodied and expansive at the same time, as she joins heaven and earth.

The other Piscean trap is escapism through various means—addiction, spaciness, avoidance, or delusion, for example. Her trouble committing to being human can lead her to the clouds, while she has trouble connecting with pragmatism, punctuality, self-care, and directness. If Pisces can develop self-awareness, boundaries, and discipline, she could become one of the world's greatest mystics—a powerful, otherworldly reminder of unconditional love and interconnection.

3

THE MOON

Our Emotions, Sensitivity, and Subconscious

THE MOON represents our inner psyche and emotional nature. Some astrologers say that the Sun is how we see ourselves, while the Moon is who we really are. Of all the planets, the Moon is the most important for us to nourish. It is the emotional backdrop for all that we do, ruling our instincts and vulnerability. A relational planet, the Moon also tells us how we receive and support loved ones. It can cause us to erupt into moodiness and overwhelming emotional intensity, but without it, we would be walking egos without complexity or depth, imagination or profundity. Shining most brightly at night, the Moon magically reflects the light of other people's Suns, pulling at our heartstrings, eliciting unconscious reactions. It is irrational but poetic and full of meaning. If we do not feed our Moon, we simply cannot feel content.

Our Moon's element, or triplicity, tells part of the story of how we feel. If our Moon falls into a water sign (Cancer, Scorpio, or Pisces), our emotions are more complex, with heightened potential for sulkiness, changeability, and dreaminess. In air signs (Gemini, Libra, or Aquarius), the Moon indicates an increased tendency toward intellectual detachment, objectivity, and communicating our feelings socially. The Moon in earth signs (Taurus, Virgo, or Capricorn) denotes steadiness, stability, pragmatism, and sometimes repression. In fire (Aries, Leo, or Sagittarius), the Moon is more direct, simple, and truthful. Bursts of emotion could lead to compulsive decisionmaking and activity.

Since fulfillment is difficult without a well-fed Moon, we might stop to consider whether our ego and personality are overriding our Moon's internal currents. For example, if we have Aquarius Moon, we must allow ourselves to experiment, shock, and express our authenticity, even if we have a more traditional Sun sign. Cancer Moon needs ample time alone and to nurture herself and others, even if her Sun sign is more adventurous. Taurus Moon must surround himself with beauty, making space to relish in pleasure, even if his Sun sign directs him toward more humanitarian pursuits.

The following chapter describes the nature of each Moon sign, along with examples of what makes each of them feel content.

MOON IN ARIES

EMOTIONAL NATURE
Honest, Assertive, Independent, Childlike

SOURCES OF CONTENTMENT
Freedom, Conquest, Leading, Passionate Expression

Aries is the most emotionally direct placement for the Moon. These Moons are marked by independence, assertiveness, and a childlike nature. There is no hiding how a Moon in Aries feels. They are honest and forthright, reacting without filtering themselves or taking the time to reflect. They know what they like, want, and feel, and go after it with fervor. Passions arise quickly, and actions soon follow. Innate warriors, Moons in Aries have the ability to endure great hardship. However, they sometimes scoff at emotional weakness and sentimental displays. To find balance, Moon in Aries must work toward compromise, making room for vulnerability and differing perspectives.

In order to feel emotionally content, Moon in Aries requires tremendous exhilaration and freedom. These Moons love to fight for and win the objects of their affection. They will initiate projects and dive headlong into adventure. Confident and outspoken, Aries Moons generate natural leaders who find their own way and become their own authority. They require regular outlets for expressing their passion, otherwise they run the risk of becoming anxious, domineering, or high-strung. At their best, Moon in Aries is exciting, honest, and bold, taking risks with great satisfaction.

MOON IN TAURUS

EMOTIONAL NATURE
Trustworthy, Stable, Security-Driven, Restrained

SOURCES OF CONTENTMENT
Earthly Pleasures, Sensuality, Predictability, Beauty

Moons in Taurus are steady and trustworthy, marked by an innate desire for comfort and security. Fertility, nurturing, and sustenance come easily to these Moons, who have the natural ability to understand their basic needs. Faithful companions and sensualists, Taurus Moons have the capacity to slow down and feel their emotions in their bodies. They have a knack for keeping their cool, remaining socially dignified and restrained, no matter their emotional state. One danger with this placement is emotional rigidity and resistance to change. Moon in Taurus can hold too tightly to personal opinions and remain in unhealthy relationships for too long. When experiencing emotional upheaval, Moons in Taurus may dig in their heels and shut down. Other times, they will find creative or sensual outlets—visiting hot springs, gardening, eating decadent food, or hosting cozy gatherings for select friends.

To feel content, Moons in Taurus must engage their artistic talents and connect with earthly pleasures. These Moons are steady and patient and do well with predictable circumstances and tangible outcomes. A beautiful home is particularly important to these creatures of comfort. Nature, food, flowers, art, and committed relationships feed their souls. While prone to stubbornness, Moons in Taurus make reliable friends and partners, helping others to savor the five senses and the beauty of the phenomenal world.

MOON IN GEMINI

EMOTIONAL NATURE
Communicative, Changeable, Analytical, Intellectual

SOURCES OF CONTENTMENT
Banter, Socializing, Good Conversations, Charming Others

At heart, Gemini is the most emotionally communicative of all Moon signs. Analyzing feelings is a favorite pastime for Gemini Moons, making them excellent writers, speakers, teachers, and counselors. Engaging conversationalists, Gemini Moon has the ability to blend heart and mind, compelling others to discuss their emotions with shared fascination. They genuinely love people, and the sentiment is usually reciprocated. Flitting from one feeling to the next, they sometimes exhaust their loved ones. Another danger is that Gemini Moons can go too far in intellectualizing their emotions. Periodically, they might remember to stop their minds and drop into their hearts and bodies more deeply.

To feel content, Gemini Moons need regular outlets for their wit, banter, and socializing. Decisive partners are ideal for these Moons, helping them to balance their fickleness and tendency toward rapidly changing emotions. Moons in Gemini want to play in the realm of language, so finding partners who are able to keep up with them mentally and conversationally helps them to feel healthy and fulfilled. At that point, they will show up at their best—imaginative, lively, charming, and adaptable.

MOON IN CANCER

Nurturing, Deep, Sensitive, Moody

SOURCES OF CONTENTMENT
Alone Time, Cooking, Being Home,
Connecting with Close Friends

The Moon rules Cancer, so this is the Moon's natural placement. Cancer and the Moon both represent motherhood, and those with Moons in Cancer are often maternal, feeling compelled to nurture those around them. Home and security are important to these tender Moons. They are most content cooking, eating, and spending time at home alone, or in the company of close friends and family. They need to find friends who share their love of staying in, and allow room for their deep currents of emotion.

A potential danger for Cancer Moons is their hypersensitivity. They are quite psychic, literally feeling other people's emotions when they walk into a room. Because they experience so much input, they are prone to moodiness and hardening, their pincers coming out to protect extreme tenderness. They do well in relationships with steady, sensible earth signs, who help to balance their moods and readily receive their maternal nurturing. These stable signs will provide ground, protection, and strength for Cancer Moons. When feeling safe, Cancer Moons shine their brightest, showing up as extraordinary creatures of caring, depth, and feeling.

MOON IN LEO

EMOTIONAL NATURE

Cheerful, Warm, Dramatic, Domineering

SOURCES OF CONTENTMENT

Attention, Creative Expression, Affection, Playfulness

Playful and affectionate, Leo Moons relish in giving and receiving love and affection. They want nothing more than to entertain their loved ones. They need to be the center of attention in relationships—the kings and queens of their personal domains. Emotionally performative, they are happiest when they have receptive audiences for their warmth and creative expression. They only have to be wary of becoming too dramatic.

At heart, Moons in Leo are cheerful, self-confident, and carefree, with an infectious quality that leads others in good times. Inspiring souls, these Moons have abundant energy that they are eager to share with everyone around them. They make loyal parents, friends, and lovers, but can sometimes become too arrogant or emotionally overbearing. When crossed, Moon in Leo has the capacity to strike back fiercely. In order to feel balanced and content, Leo Moon must return to his natural dignity and creativity. This way he will show up at his best—a benevolent leader who is generous, warm, and full of heart.

MOON IN VIRGO

EMOTIONAL NATURE

Practical, Humble, Helpful, Critical

SOURCES OF CONTENTMENT

Organization, Serving Others, Safety, Analyzing Feelings

Moon in Virgo indicates a helpful, sensible, and analytical emotional nature, which can sometimes teeter into coldness and detachment. Virgo is a logical sign for an illogical planet, and Virgo Moon can sometimes suffer from lack of emotional flexibility—easily hurt, shy, and critical of others. They want to be perfect and sometimes struggle with expressing messier emotions. However, they are humble souls, committed to self-improvement and developing their emotional awareness. Loyal and dependable friends, they offer practical detachment in the midst of emotional upheavals. Their simplicity and innocence can provide a welcome respite from life's complications. They are able to talk things through in detail, unafraid of emotional work and communication.

Virgo Moons feel most content when they have established healthy boundaries and regular outlets for serving others. They thrive with meaningful work and people to devote themselves to, who will reciprocate with appreciation and respect for their intelligence and efforts. These Moons only have to be sure they are practicing self-respect, never surrendering their needs to another's or nitpicking others out of fear of inferiority. The more they ease up on self-criticism, the more fluid their lives will become. At that point, their warm, affectionate nature rises to the surface, surprising you with playfulness, warmth, and sensitivity. They will shine as the beacons of purity and devotion that they are, eagerly helping anyone in need.

MOON IN LIBRA

EMOTIONAL NATURE
Adaptable, Balanced, Artistic, People-Pleasing

SOURCES OF CONTENTMENT
Beauty, Balance, Stillness, Peace

Libra Moons are peaceful and polite, fearing confrontation. Diplomatic, friendly, and open, Libra Moons can balance the emotional disharmony of loved ones, making space for their fullest expression. At times, Libra Moons can fail to stand up for what they want, or to even know what that is. Wanting to be liked by everyone, their charm and social grace can veer into people-pleasing. They can become dishonest, morphing into whoever you want them to be, which may cause confusion for those close to them. However, Moons in Libra can be incredibly lovely friends if accepted for who they are—romantic, adaptable, and, at times, indefinable.

For Libra Moons to feel content, they would do well establishing domestic tranquility, as they crave beauty, stillness, and balanced partnerships. Romantic gestures are common for Libra Moons, who possess great potential to demonstrate emotions through their art, poetry, and design. In fact, Libra Moons are likely to be artistic and musical, or at least patrons of the arts. Sensitive to harmony and grace, their gentle hearts yearn for the magic of aesthetic refinement in all of its expressions—lush gardens, sensitive artworks, harmonious music, and elegant decor. These are the domains where they become more forthright—their uncertainty peeling away into leadership as they guide others into creativity, partnership, and love.

MOON IN SCORPIO

EMOTIONAL NATURE
Passionate, Deep, Wise, Destructive

SOURCES OF CONTENTMENT
Magic, Profundity, Extremism, Inner Exploration

No one is more passionate and mysterious than Moon in Scorpio. Emotionally intense, these Moons would thrive on a path of psychological transformation. These deep and brooding souls have vast potentials for awakening wisdom. Emotionally fearless, Scorpio Moon understands all facets of human experience—the dark, forbidden, taboo undercurrents that many of us are afraid to feel or even mention. Sensitive and perceptive, Scorpio Moons can make excellent healers and shamans, able to guide others into their forgotten corners—supporting them in opening cellar doors of pain and childhood trauma. Intimate and intuitive, they can see right through people, sometimes using this for emotional manipulation. Their biggest journey is learning to balance emotional extremes, remembering not to act on every feeling or collapse into intensity.

Scorpio Moons derive contentment from working through jealousy, obsession, and control, balancing their emotional extremism, and allowing others to be exactly as they are. Scorpio Moons are well served finding partners who are unafraid of plunging into the depths of intimacy with them. They would feel satisfied in careers helping people in prisons, poverty, or facing death. They would also make excellent midwives and doulas, guiding mothers and babies through the process of birth. At their best, these are profound and magical souls who help the rest of us to face ourselves while glimpsing the unknown.

MOON IN SAGITTARIUS

EMOTIONAL NATURE
Forthright, Restless, Enthusiastic, Optimistic

SOURCES OF CONTENTMENT
Travel, Teaching, Adventure, Nature

Moon in Sagittarius indicates a restless, freedom-loving, and outspoken emotional nature. Explorers, these souls are naturally cheerful and friendly, easily making new acquaintances. However, these Moons can struggle with intimacy and depth, finding it difficult to grow roots and remain tied down. Speaking before they think, they are known for their frankness and candor, sometimes seeming rude in their commitment to truth. Excellent speakers and teachers, Sagittarius Moons easily educate and inspire.

To find contentment, physical exertion is key for Sagittarius Moons, as it provides an outlet for their antsy, unsettled energy. In fact, they can become passionate athletes and masters of body-wisdom practices such as yoga, tai chi, or qigong. At heart, they love philosophy and travel and feel fulfilled visiting faraway places—or at least learning about them. They enjoy nature and exploring other cultures and religions. They also love sharing the wisdom that they glean from their explorations. Excellent travel companions, they infuse others with optimism and enthusiasm. They thrive with fixed sign partners, who help to anchor their restless spirits. If given the freedom to continue wandering, their hearts remain full, and they will help expand the horizons of their friends and companions—offering an unfettered, optimistic outlook, lovingly and freely.

MOON IN CAPRICORN

EMOTIONAL NATURE

Conservative, Virtuous, Serious, Reserved

SOURCES OF CONTENTMENT

Music, Family, Comedy, Networking

Moon in Capricorn generates a conservative, dependable, and reserved emotional nature. Controlling their emotions, Capricorn Moons avoid public displays of passion or inappropriateness. They are unlikely to explode or lose their cool in front of others. However, they must work hard to soften their hearts, releasing repression and feeling the full spectrum of emotion, without judgment. Dutiful and family-oriented, Capricorn Moons work hard to create security. They yearn to be integral parts of society—ambitious, dignified, and socially respected. Sensitive to timing, music and comedy could be helpful outlets for their emotional expression. Capricorn Moons have huge hearts, and they must find healthy outlets for their serious, responsible side so it doesn't obstruct their openness and warmth.

The key to contentment for Capricorn Moons is allowing themselves to orient toward business and family, becoming successful, powerful, and driven, while at the same time working toward a more fluid emotional expression. They would do well in partnerships with water signs who help to saturate their rigidness with watery nurturing, granting them permission to relax and feel their hearts. Capricorn Moons are on a journey to learning that emotions are nothing to fear. If they can master this, they will become more balanced—composed and self-sufficient, while also compassionate and true.

MOON IN AQUARIUS

EMOTIONAL NATURE
Unconventional, Rebellious, Authentic, Detached

SOURCES OF CONTENTMENT
Invention, Community, Creative Work, Humanitarianism

Moon in Aquarius generates a rebellious soul—creative, ingenious, and unconventional. Aquarius Moon can sometimes create emotional chaos, seeking conflict, knowing intuitively that it could lead to awakening. Uncomfortable with stagnancy and disingenuousness, Aquarius Moon will force others to be authentic, pushing them to their edge, sometimes with shock. At times, Aquarius Moons can scare people with volcanic eruptions of emotion and combativeness. However, they are unlikely to hold grudges, processing and releasing intense exchanges quickly. This is the best placement to move on from heartbreak, as they feel everything suddenly and fully then let it go.

The key to Aquarius Moons' contentedness is having a healthy outlet for their eccentricity, feeling free to invent and rebel, create community, and orient toward fringe pursuits, technology, and the future. Fascinating conversationalists and friends, Aquarius Moons must work to extend their love for humanity to individuals, as they sometimes become too cool and detached when relating on an intimate level. If they work consciously with their detachment, it can become their gift. Excellent therapists and counselors, they can harness their creativity and objectivity to help others work through difficult emotions. Unafraid of chaos, they won't flinch in the midst of challenging situations. They thrive with friends and partners who allow them to be their idiosyncratic selves, and who appreciate occasional jolts of electricity.

MOON IN PISCES

EMOTIONAL NATURE
Compassionate, Imaginative, Loving, Lacking Boundaries

SOURCES OF CONTENTMENT
Dreaming, the Arts, Spirituality, the Ocean

The dreamiest of placements, Moon in Pisces makes for an imaginative soul, who loves to escape into fantasy. Ever compassionate, Moons in Pisces could love almost anyone. Extremely sensitive, they can psychically intuit the feelings of others. Pisces Moon understands all of human experience, their emotional nature encompassing every sign of the zodiac.

To feel content, meditation and spirituality feed a Pisces Moon. Photography, film, and improvisational dance and music would all be worthy and natural pursuits. The danger for Pisces Moon is their potential escapism and victimization. Maintaining healthy emotional boundaries and staying rooted in reality are important skills to develop. They would do well in friendships with earthier signs who can help them relate to the more practical aspects of reality. Then they can be at their best—optimistic and loving, with boundless sympathy, able to understand the hearts of even the most vile and downtrodden among us. With their otherworldly presence and gentleness, they can show the rest of us how to open to transcendent love, untethered to the arbitrary constraints of the material world.

4

THE ASCENDANT

Our Outermost Layer, First Impression, and Physical Appearance

OUR ASCENDANT, or Rising sign, is the entry point into our whole life and being, coloring the rest of our lives and natal chart. It describes our outermost layer and how we make a first impression. If the Sun is how we see ourselves and the Moon is how we really are, then the Ascendant is how others see us. Literally, it is the beginning of our astrological chart, pointing to the easternmost horizon at the moment of our first breath. Along with our Sun and Moon signs, the Ascendant is fundamental in painting the portrait of who we are. It tells us about the masks that we wear and the more superficial aspects of ourselves. Yet these are important elements of our personality, key indicators of how we show up in our daily lives, they describe how we relate to coworkers, acquaintances, and friends.

The most important point in our chart, the Ascendant isn't simply an indication of our outer traits. It also reveals our shadow selves, aspects of our childhood, likely partnerships, and how we find balance. For example, people see Aquarius Ascendants as iconoclastic, exciting, and erratic. In childhood, they may feel like aliens or outsiders, defining themselves by their differentness. To find balance, these Ascendants must integrate playfulness and warmth with their cool rebellion. Often, they attract Leo-like partners who will help them with this balance. After all, Leo is opposite to Aquarius.

Governing our body, style, and appearance, the Ascendant also indicates our physical features and the way that we carry ourselves. Libra Rising indicates charm, a melodic voice, and good style; Gemini Rising signifies sparkling, inquisitive eyes, and a tendency to talk with our hands; and Scorpio Rising appears dark and mysterious, investigating new people with intensity.

The following chapter describes the nature of each Ascendant, their first impression, childhood, physical features, and how they find balance.

ARIES ASCENDANT

FIRST IMPRESSION
Confident, Strong, Courageous, Direct

PHYSICAL APPEARANCE
High Foreheads, Commanding Stature,
Darting Eyes, Prone to Head Injuries, Possible Birthmarks
or Scars on Their Heads or Faces

Individuals with Aries Ascendants come across as strong, straightforward, confident, and enthusiastic. This is the strongest placement for the Ascendant with Aries, the beginning of the zodiac falling at the beginning of a person's chart. In their daily lives, these Ascendants have an easy time directly stating their points of view, asserting themselves, and asking for what they want. Swift and decisive, they possess natural leadership abilities. They like to initiate projects and take charge, becoming catalytic forces in every endeavor. Ruled by Mars, planet of virility, sexuality, and athleticism, these Ascendants are often athletes, able to easily rouse their physical energies.

CHILDHOOD

As children, Aries Ascendants are rambunctious and enthusiastic. They quickly become self-reliant, learning who they are apart from family dynamics. Their defining trajectory is to become free of their parents, independent and in charge of their own lives. This begins in childhood, carrying over well into adulthood. Difficulties may arise early in life since they have the tendency to overshoot and act with excessive vigor. However, they have great stores of personal power and self-expression, which are keys to unlocking their vast potential. These children are not afraid to fight for what they want, relishing challenges without fear. Later in life, they are capable of great self-sacrifice, undergoing hardship for their families in sometimes-heroic ways.

FINDING BALANCE

Aries Ascendants can be argumentative and pugnacious. Their balance lies in incorporating the qualities of Libra—their shadow self and polar opposite. These qualities include tact, carefulness, and consideration of others. They often attract Libra-like partners who help them curb their rashness and self-absorption. If they manage to blend their innate sense of independence with their strong desire to connect, they then can hold peaceful and respectful space for friends and partners. This way, they will develop harmony in their relationships, which is deeply fulfilling for Aries Ascendants—a signpost of their evolution.

TAURUS ASCENDANT

Attractive, Dependable, Slow, Sensual

Serene Eyes, Delicate Jawlines, Prominent Necks
(Thick or Long and Elegant), Larger Bodies

Taurus is one of the most likable placements for the Ascendant. Others see these Ascendants as beautiful and attractive, regardless of how they look. They present well, with good style, steady demeanors, and natural displays of richness. Peaceful and easygoing, they magnetize many friends. They are likely to be talented dancers, gardeners, cooks, ceramicists, or stylists, enjoying arts that are beautiful, tactile, and practical. Taurus Ascendants take their time to feel their environments, appreciating luxury and the finer aspects of life. Uncomfortable with change, they prefer predictability and to operate in the realm of tangibles. They also enjoy connecting with others through the sense pleasures, mutually appreciating good food, wine, sex, and other indulgences. They allow ample time to rest and take care of themselves, which indicates healthy self-worth. They only have to be wary of stubbornness and forming opinions that are too fixed. They can lack the ability to go with the flow, resisting changing tides and differing opinions.

CHILDHOOD

Taurus Ascendants are serene, calm, and patient children, who sometimes require gentle persuasion in order to make transitions. They move slowly, and sometimes have trouble adapting to abrupt change. Taurus Ascendants' early lives are often marked by comfort, stability, and security. Their families may instill the belief that accumulating wealth and material objects are important pursuits, which could generate overly materialistic outlooks. They may also learn to associate food with comfort, having to work toward curbing overeating and excessive indulgence later in life. However, the security they experience in childhood allows them to be generous and maternal creatures. They are able to include others in their natural radiance, as they effortlessly exude comfort and safety.

FINDING BALANCE

The lesson for Taurus Rising comes from letting go, embracing change, and diving into the less tangible aspects of human experience. They must express their sexuality and sensuality openly, finding partners who will relish physical pleasure with them. Their shadow side is Scorpio (their polar opposite), and they must learn to integrate the darker aspects of their psyche—such as possessiveness, jealousy, and anguish. This normally comes to them through relationships with more intense partners, who disrupt their sense of security while deepening their emotional journey. Their lifelong path involves diving into the unknown, merging their inherent grace, practicality, and aesthetic proclivities with the unstable realm of emotional depth.

GEMINI ASCENDANT

FIRST IMPRESSION
Social, Witty, Adaptable, Intelligent

PHYSICAL APPEARANCE
Delicate Features, Naturally Slim and Agile, Mischievous Twinkle in the Eyes, Jittery, Talk with the Hands, Expressive Faces

Gemini Ascendants come across as intelligent and witty, possessing strong minds and social graces. Communication is key for these

Ascendants, who thrive when connecting with others and participating actively in society. Excellent teachers, they are adept at chatting, exchanging ideas, and sharing all that they've learned. Acquiring a variety of interests and trades, Gemini Ascendants must sometimes work toward mastering one subject. They have insatiable curiosities, gathering pieces of information wherever they go. Inquisitive and restless, they love to meet many people, asking them questions with genuine interest. With so much to explore, it can be difficult for these Ascendants to settle down or commit to one place, person, or career.

CHILDHOOD

Gemini Ascendants require a lot of stimulation. They are wiggly and communicative babies—curious souls who need extra supervision. Talkative and intelligent, these children must fulfill their desire to communicate with the world and to learn voraciously. They often seem younger than their classmates and carry this youthfulness into adulthood. These children are best served when allowed to connect frequently with others, talking and socializing with many people. This helps them to develop their innate adaptability.

FINDING BALANCE

Prone to nervous tension, Gemini Ascendants must work consciously with their impatience and boredom, finding physical outlets for heightened mental energy. They feel fulfilled with constant stimulation—new experiences, travels, and connections. Relationships with Sagittarian-like partners (their polar opposite) will help them to expand their intellectual minds. Philosophical and spiritual souls will deepen

Gemini Ascendants' experience, imbuing trivial information with context and meaning. For Gemini Ascendants to find balance and expand their tremendous gifts, they must seek wisdom, explore unfamiliar cultures and thought systems, and connect more fully with their bodies and hearts.

CANCER ASCENDANT

FIRST IMPRESSION
Maternal, Nurturing, Emotional, Sensitive

PHYSICAL APPEARANCE
Round Faces, Prominent Stomach (Very Round or
Very Chiseled), Puffed Out Chests, Dreamy Expressions

Cancer Ascendants are typically seen as nurturing and caring souls who readily demonstrate their sensitivity and emotionalism. These Ascendants are quite psychic, with powerful intuitions and the ability to feel the emotions of others as their own. As such, these creatures sometimes develop hard outer shells to protect their vulnerability. Rather than making their tenderness apparent, they come off as sharp or moody. Establishing a safe and secure home is vital for these Ascendants as it will take the place of their hardened shell. Particularly sensitive, they are best suited to clean, peaceful environments. Able to work well with the public, Cancer Ascendants are often good businesspeople, possessing determination, practicality, and caution, along with strong intuition. Loyal to close friends, they enjoy nurturing and cooking for others. They like to connect deeply, preferring intimacy over superficiality. When they feel safe, these Ascendants can travel well, carrying their homes on their backs while adapting easily to changing currents.

CHILDHOOD

The relationship to the mother is particularly significant for Cancer Rising children, who typically feel quite attached to their caregivers. Because of this, it is especially important that they develop healthy relationships with their parents. Quiet children, they take in their environments through permeable walls, adapting themselves to other people's moods and expectations. This is the seed of their deeply intuitive nature. They watch everyone around them, learning to trust themselves as their hunches match with reality. An important part of their childhood journey is to let go of their deep dependencies on their families. They must learn how to self-protect and become more autonomous.

FINDING BALANCE

Establishing boundaries is key for Cancer Ascendants. With a strong nurturing drive, they easily feel lost in other people's emotions. They must learn that, ultimately, we are not responsible for anyone else. In the end, we must find our own way. These Ascendants tend to cling to their emotions and the past. Part of their trajectory involves developing a steadier sense of rhythm and timing. This happens to be the gift of Capricorn, their polar opposite. Cancer Ascendants typically seek partners who embody Capricornian strength and stability, which helps them feel safe and secure. But first, they must develop these qualities within themselves. As they build healthier containers for their watery emotions, they will be able to flow more freely—nurturing and protecting others while mastering their gift of deep intuition.

LEO ASCENDANT

Playful, Creative, Dramatic, Affectionate

Distinctive Mane of Hair, Dramatic Expression, Regal Posture

Leo Ascendants shine when they walk into a room, expressing a star quality and dramatic flair. Their lives are oriented toward creativity and unearthing their talents. These Ascendants require much admiration and respect to feel okay about themselves, although they're reluctant to admit it. They are warm, gifted, and generous souls who want to share their light and lead others in good times. Playful and fun people, they enjoy socializing, requiring regular outlets for their spontaneity, inspiration, creativity, and passion.

CHILDHOOD

Naturally popular, Leo Ascendant children do well with their peers, fitting in while becoming leaders of their friend groups. Early on, Leo Ascendants often receive either too little attention or too much—sometimes a combination of both. This drives their desire to be seen and adored. If they work consciously with this, they will begin to feel more fulfilled, relying less on the approval of others. Parents might encourage Leo Ascendants' uniqueness in order to curb their fear of standing out as different or weird. The more they are able to express themselves creatively, the easier their lives will become as adults.

In their desire to feel accepted and loved, Leo Ascendants can forget to foster their individuality and authenticity. They have to work toward expressing themselves freely, without worrying what other people think. Dismantling their fear of rejection and need for validation will lead them to feeling more whole and secure. Aquarian-like people are wonderful partners for Leo Rising souls, as they are naturally fearless, rebellious spirits with humanitarian outlooks. Incorporating these qualities gives Leo Ascendants a broader sense of purpose and self-assuredness, which is vital for them to develop a healthy self-expression.

VIRGO ASCENDANT

FIRST IMPRESSION
Humble, Helpful, Innocent, Shy

PHYSICAL APPEARANCE
Graceful and Gentle Movements, Soft-Spoken, Refined Noses, Clear Eyes, Delicate-Looking but Strong Bodies

Virgo Ascendants are polite and soft-spoken, caring greatly for the welfare of others. They are humble and devoted, orienting toward helping people. With ample discernment, they can easily size up a room, along with everyone in it. Analytical and perceptive, they notice small details, with a penchant for recognizing disingenuousness. Cleanliness and order are important for these sensitive souls to feel good and productive. They only have to try and curb their critical bite, along with a tendency to self-sacrifice.

CHILDHOOD

Virgo Ascendants are sweet, obedient children who would never hurt a fly. Prone to worrying, they do well connecting with nature and small animals and learning self-acceptance. Perfectionistic parents are detrimental to these souls, who need to learn that it's okay to make mistakes, relax, and develop their imaginations. Romantic books and mysteries are appealing to these children, helping them to assuage their rigidity and open to the more fluid realm of dreams and fantasy—to which they are very drawn.

FINDING BALANCE

For Virgo Ascendants, the key to finding balance is to ease up on judgment, learning to forgive themselves and others. Self-effacing and sensitive even to slight criticisms, these Ascendants must work toward mastering unconditional self-love and -care. Prone to digestive issues and delicate nervous systems, they would benefit from tending to their health—as long as they don't overdo it. Meditation, yoga, and music are helpful activities for easing tension, helping them to turn off their analytical minds. Their shadow self is Pisces (their polar opposite), so incorporating the Fish's qualities will help them to evolve greatly. They are drawn to watery and poetic souls who naturally accept everyone, go with the flow, and demonstrate the power of limitless compassion. Defying logic, their Piscean counterparts help them to ease up on perfectionism, teaching them that everything—including the Virgo Ascendant—is perfect exactly the way it is.

LIBRA ASCENDANT

FIRST IMPRESSION
Charming, Graceful, Indecisive, Peacemaking

PHYSICAL APPEARANCE
Small Symmetrical Features, Melodic Voice, Bright Smile,
Heart-Shaped Face, Dimples, Good Style

Libra Ascendants are attractive and charming, carrying themselves with beauty and grace. They will harmonize a room as soon as they enter it—noticing energies that are off-balance and restoring them to equilibrium. Justice and diplomacy are important to these souls, who try their best to remain fair-minded and objective. Seeing both sides of any circumstance, they can struggle with making decisions, wavering in vacillation. Sensitive to harmony and aesthetics, these Ascendants often dress beautifully and are able to create environments that are pleasing and refined. Excellent negotiators, listeners, and counselors, their sense of fairness and openness is immediate and pronounced. Identifying strongly with their relationships, they place tremendous weight on finding the perfect partner. Laziness and complacency are possible until they know exactly what they want—and often until they've found a fulfilling partnership. Compatible with almost anyone, they could struggle to find the right person. Often idealizing others, they can lack in discernment.

CHILDHOOD

Libra Ascendants are kind, peaceful, and cooperative children, who are usually quite popular. Charming, they learn early on how to have their way, but they do so in a gentle, nonaggressive manner. It would help these children to encourage their self-assertiveness and to teach them that it's okay to displease people at times. Living in a peaceful environment is particularly important for these sensitive children, helping to lift their moods and stabilize their delicate equilibriums. Rallying them to action can be difficult, so gentle but firm parenting styles can be most effective.

FINDING BALANCE

Libra Ascendants must work through their tendency toward inaction and laziness. This stems from two things—their desire to please people and their ability to see the good in every potential. In fact, Libra Ascendants often become frustrated by their own uncertainty. Their balance lies in learning to feel their hearts and trust their feelings and decisions. Balancing their masculinity and femininity is also vital—finding the sweet spot between intellect and intuition, mind and heart, assertiveness and receptivity. Their shadow side is aggressive Aries (their polar opposite). They are drawn to Aries-like partners who are more daring, impulsive, and straightforward, helping them become more courageous and decisive and express themselves more directly. As Libra Ascendants develop more confidence, their innate inquisitiveness opens them to diverse experiences. They begin to dive headlong into their creative and romantic adventures, without second-guessing.

SCORPIO ASCENDANT

FIRST IMPRESSION
Magnetic, Intense, Powerful, Dark

PHYSICAL APPEARANCE
Piercing Eyes, Direct Gaze, Mysterious Demeanor,
Often-Pale Skin, Powerful Physique

People see Scorpio Ascendants as powerful, secretive, and determined, demonstrating immense magnetism and charisma. These Ascendants are survivors who can handle intense situations. They are able to transform circumstances and energies by their very presence. Agents of change in the world, they hold much persuasiveness and influence. Formidable opponents, these are not people you would want to cross. They are willful and resilient, often becoming effective businesspeople and leaders, applying their thoroughness and resolve to any challenge. With their powerful intuition they can see right through us. Natural investigators, they could make excellent therapists or scientists. Scorpio Ascendants wear their depth on their sleeve, intimidating others with their steady eyes and penetrating gaze. They usually keep their emotions under wraps, but they will sometimes explode with emotional outbursts, teetering into extremes. Their greatest gift is their emotional fearlessness—their ability to plunge into the depths and lead others toward intimacy and revelation.

CHILDHOOD

As children, Scorpio Ascendants may seem reserved, feeling deeply while not expressing it. Displays of unconditional love are important for these children, who could feel especially fearful of being misunderstood. They are fascinating and magnetic creatures, conveying depth well beyond their age. Strong-willed and stubborn, they are likely to fight and win, even against their parents. Prone to childhood trauma, it is imperative to surround these children with supportive peers and adults who will help them nurture their gifts of perception. It would benefit these Ascendants to orient their obsessive nature toward healthy pursuits.

FINDING BALANCE

To find balance, Scorpio Ascendants must learn how to trust and surrender, relinquishing their need for control. Developing steadiness could be helpful in unlocking their gifts—deepening their abilities of transformation and perception without falling off-kilter. They often attract Taurus-like partners (their polar opposite) who teach them simplicity and steadiness. Practical, even-keeled partners show them how to be still and take care of themselves—eating good food, practicing yoga, gardening, and luxuriating. This would temper Scorpio Ascendants' tendency toward extremism and complication. As they find their sweet spot, these Ascendants could make great strides toward changing the world, helping to transmute the darkest corners of reality from the ground of inner security, worthiness, and dependability.

SAGITTARIUS ASCENDANT

FIRST IMPRESSION
Cheerful, Optimistic, Inspiring, Restless

PHYSICAL APPEARANCE
Haphazard Grace, Friendly Open Faces,
Strong Legs, Pointy Chins (Like the Centaur),
Comedic Expressions, Sparkling Eyes

Sagittarius Ascendants are cheerful, outgoing, independent, and uplifting. Ruled by Jupiter, the "great benefic," these Ascendants generate tremendous luck, stumbling upon good fortune and auspicious coincidences wherever they go. Restless, they crave adventure, frequently traveling both physically and in the mind. Humorous and happy-go-lucky, they sometimes avoid difficult emotions, feeling burdened by other people's problems (and even their own). Spiritual souls, they love the outdoors, tuning in to the higher realms when immersed in nature. They can sometimes come across as blunt or tactless, dedicating themselves firmly to speaking the truth. These inspiring Ascendants can make wonderful teachers—opening people's minds to different perspectives, expanding their consciousness as they continuously expand their own.

CHILDHOOD

Sagittarius Rising children are playful and joyful, displaying sunny dispositions. They are often funny, telling jokes and generating laughter. They might learn to refrain from saying exactly what is on their minds, becoming more sensitive to how their words affect others. However, their freshness is inspiring. These imaginative children will readily connect with symbolism, spirit, and magic. They do well with frequent physical activity and time in nature. Outgoing and freedom loving, they thrive when allowed to follow their curiosity and yearning for adventure.

FINDING BALANCE

Sagittarius Ascendants seek truth and want to discover it on their own terms. They may seem antsy in their constant search for experience and meaning, which sometimes leads to overzealousness and recklessness. They would feel more balanced developing their Gemini qualities (their polar opposite). Discriminating, practical, and cynical, Gemini helps to counter Sagittarius Ascendants' broadmindedness and naive optimism. In fact, Sagittarius Ascendants often find partners who are Gemini-like and intellectual, helping them create more cohesive frameworks for their abundance of expansive ideas and goals. This helps them to increase their analytical focus and refine their perspectives. This way, they can lead the rest of us to wisdom through their well-planned adventures, both in the world and in our minds.

CAPRICORN ASCENDANT

FIRST IMPRESSION
Reserved, Serious, Determined, Refined

PHYSICAL APPEARANCE
Deep Voice, Wise Eyes, Slow and Deliberate, Strong Teeth,
Prominent Eyebrows, Well-Defined Jawline

Capricorn Ascendants come across as traditional and patient people: timid, restrained, and a bit inhibited. Mindful of decency and decorum, they are cautious about rocking the boat and breaking from societal norms. People may mistake them as snobby or aloof, but they are actually prone to feeling insecure, yearning to express themselves more freely. However, their restraint is also their asset, producing elegant and refined individuals. Capricorn Ascendants are wonderfully trustworthy, determined, and self-sufficient. They can be funny and musically talented, since they have an excellent sense of timing. Able to accomplish any task, they must only be wary of their stifling perfectionism. Stable and focused, Capricorn Ascendants will move carefully, demonstrating the wisdom of the Goat—placing one foot in front of the other, slowly but surely climbing any mountain.

CHILDHOOD

Capricorn Ascendants are often timid and pensive children. They seem wise beyond their years—little adults in children's bodies. They are strongly connected to their parents, and especially the father. Sometimes they experience a disruption to one of their parental relationships, which can lead to prominent feelings of isolation and loneliness as children. If encouraged to play more, this could offset their deep sense of responsibility and order. These Ascendants become younger as they age, their sense of humor finding stronger expression as their seriousness begins to soften.

FINDING BALANCE

Capricorn Ascendants can struggle with the belief that hardship and obstacles are necessary to achieve their goals. Feelings of guilt and repression could hold them back, preventing them from opening to life's pleasures. Their balance comes from developing Cancerian qualities (their polar opposite). They must connect with both their inner mother and unconditional love, which help wash away self-imposed limitations. They are quite loving and sensitive in close relationships, and they do well with maternal partners who help to penetrate their stiffer exteriors. Humor, intimacy, and ease are fully available to this dependable sign, if they can work consciously with their shadow—blending their feminine and masculine selves, and learning that it is okay to be sloppy and imperfect. Their innate humor will shine through when they learn to enjoy themselves as they nobly dedicate their lives to family and career.

AQUARIUS ASCENDANT

FIRST IMPRESSION
Creative, Independent, Funny, Quirky

PHYSICAL APPEARANCE
Nice Profile, Eccentric Movements, Light Eyes, Shapely Legs,
Soft-Spoken or Outspoken, Sensitive to Temperature

Aquarius Ascendants show up as eccentric, rebellious, and exciting souls, who easily make people laugh with their unusual perspectives. Sometimes they seem obstinate in their insistence on doing things differently and thinking outside the box. With unique style and an unusual demeanor, these Ascendants keep us on our toes, shocking us with nonconformity. Intuition and impulse are strong for these Ascendants, who will flash on answers and insights that seem to come from outer space. They do best when they are able to express themselves authentically and freely, without feeling restrained or judged. While they sometimes seem cold or aloof, these Ascendants thrive when part of strong communities and humanitarian pursuits. They are able to establish interesting and creative friend groups with niche interests that bind them together. Visionaries and iconoclasts, they can easily see the bigger picture. They pave the way to the future, helping establish a society that reflects the pinnacle of human potential.

CHILDHOOD

Aquarian Rising children are friendly and gregarious. Inhabiting fascinating worlds of their own creation, they have little need for social acceptance. These are children who bring home exotic lizards and peculiar friends, thriving in their explorations into the unknown. They may seem aloof since they prefer the realm of ideas and imagination to emotional connection. At times, they could suffer from feeling alienated from their peers, but this is also their gift. They are able to discover their unique fingerprint, showing up as their authentic selves, no matter the circumstances.

FINDING BALANCE

While Aquarius Ascendants are wildly idiosyncratic and special souls, they find balance when they've established an audience for their unique talents—blending their warmth and creativity with deeper purpose. Allowing for more passion and emotional displays is healthy for these detached Ascendants. They have to learn that outbursts of emotion are laced with joy and love, and that this genuine expression can bind us together altruistically. Finding loving, expressive, dramatic partners who embody Leo-like qualities (their polar opposite) will help these Ascendants connect more deeply with the human experience, anchoring their alien gifts to the earth for the benefit of all.

PISCES ASCENDANT

FIRST IMPRESSION
Easygoing, Imaginative, Sensitive, Impractical

PHYSICAL APPEARANCE
Large Dreamy Eyes, Gentle Demeanor, Soothing Voice,
Prominent Feet, Soft Skin, Flowing Movements, Star Quality

Those with Pisces Ascendant have the special ability to blend with their surroundings. They can become the life of the party as they merge effortlessly with the energies of the room. Their primary entry point into the world is through their idealism and sensitivity. They are often creative and spiritual, enjoying highly imaginative arts—such as photography, film, dance, music, and drama. Chameleons, these rising signs can take on the personalities of those around them, moving like water to accommodate anyone's twists and shapes. Magical, gentle, and soothing, these otherworldly creatures draw people into their deeply loving presence.

CHILDHOOD

Pisces Rising children are perceptive and dreamy, needing ample time alone to live in the realm of imagination. If these sensitive beings are not protected, they will absorb other people's emotions, becoming psychic sponges for negativity. Pretending like everything is okay when their parents are fighting will harm Pisces-Ascendant children. They are extremely sensitive and will literally feel other people's emotions. Meditation and other methods of self-care are good to begin early on so they can harness their gifts of sensitivity and compassion without feeling overwhelmed.

FINDING BALANCE

To find balance, Pisces Ascendants must develop good boundaries, realism, and groundedness. These are Virgoan qualities—their polar opposite. Permeable and idealistic, Pisces Ascendants sometimes find it difficult to keep their feet on the ground and stay on task. They are attracted to Virgo-like partners who've mastered the art of being in the world—taking care of their health, balancing the budget, and maintaining a strong work ethic. While Pisces Ascendants are mysterious, poetic, and alluring, they are drawn to those who can exist in mundane reality. Rational, logical partners will help to anchor these ethereal souls, curbing their tendency toward escapism and disassociation. When they've found center, they will be quite adept at moving between realms, helping others to connect to art, dreams, and spirituality in practical, high-minded, and helpful ways.

5

THE INNER PLANETS

Mercury, Venus, and Mars

A S WE PEEL BACK the layers of who we are, we arrive at the inner planets—Mercury, Venus, and Mars. Also known as the personal planets, these celestial bodies orbit closest to Earth and represent the main facets of our basic personality—specifically our minds, our love nature, and our drives. Mercury rules the mind, intellect, and communication; Venus rules our love nature, values, and creativity; and Mars rules our physical exertion, attractions, and sexuality.

Where these planets fall reveals how we express these basic energies. Someone with Mercury in Gemini would be witty and intellectual, with an agile mind and a strong ability to communicate. Venus in Libra reveals a proclivity for art and romance—a flirtatious and aesthetically sensitive soul. Mars in Leo indicates sexual confidence and playfulness, as well as the tendency to initiate creative projects.

We are all beautifully intricate. Learning about our inner planets, we discover language to describe our everyday complexities and inconsistencies. For example, people who seem serious and restrained upon first impression (Capricorn Rising) could also feel pulled to pursue wild adventures and experiences (Sagittarius Moon). Someone who draws in deep, mysterious souls (Scorpio Venus) could feel more attracted to witty intellectuals (Gemini Mars).

Thus we begin our journey of learning about the planets, beginning with the closest ones and working our way out. After learning about the inner planets in this chapter, we will delve into the social and outer planets, which become increasingly more complex the further we move away from Earth.

MERCURY
THE MIND AND COMMUNICATION

The planet Mercury rules the mind, communication, and intellect. Our Mercury sign indicates how we speak, learn, write, and reason. Describing our analytical minds, the position of Mercury in our chart tells us how we exchange ideas and assimilate information. Ruling our curiosity and interests, it can also point to the subjects we are likely to study. Since Mercury rules speech, it can even predict the sound of our voices.

Are we adept storytellers? Slow but careful learners? Drawn to studying philosophy and religion? History and antiques? Do we speak forcefully or humbly? These are the types of questions our Mercury placement begins to answer.

For example, Mercury in Leo produces natives (people with this placement) who are comfortable with performing and public speaking. Those with Mercury in Scorpio enjoy deep and intimate conversations; they enjoy taking things apart in order to understand them. Mercury in Libras use beautiful language and melodic speech; possessing fair and balanced minds, they tend to study law or the arts.

At its worst, Mercury can be fickle and superficial, its innate curiosity leading to insatiability. Intellectual gifts can lose their connection with heart, turning into prejudices, rationalization, and speediness. At its best, Mercury is the messenger and the mirror, relaying information with clarity and precision, which connects us with one another. Associated with the Greek god Hermes, the sandal-winged messenger of gods, Mercury flies between the human and higher realms, so we can gather knowledge to assimilate into wisdom and awakening.

The following section describes Mercury in each sign, including styles of communication, intellectual interests, and patterns of speech.

MERCURY IN ARIES

Mercury in Aries natives are assertive and forceful, with a direct style of communication. They have impatient minds, sometimes glossing over details. They often come across as more combative than they actually feel. However, childlike innocence and charm infuse their speech, helping to temper their aggressiveness. Talented at initiating projects and self-promotion, they are often drawn to business and entrepreneurialism. They only have to work on developing follow-through, as they tend to enjoy starting things more than finishing.

MERCURY IN TAURUS

Mercury in Taurus natives are methodical thinkers, taking their time to make decisions. Once they do, they are quite decisive and even stubborn. While they can be slow to initiate projects, when they put their minds to something, they are incredibly dependable and thorough. One of their gifts is common sense, as they are able to think pragmatically, within the realm of tangibles. Kinesthetic learners, they do particularly well retaining information when the five senses are involved. In fact, they may study culinary arts, farming, dance, flower arranging, or fashion—any subject that involves the sense pleasures and their refined, artistic tastes. They speak slowly and with purpose. Straightforward, no-nonsense, and authoritative, people tend to take these natives seriously. They also have a pleasant style of speech. They are often talented singers, known for their beautiful and soothing voices.

MERCURY IN GEMINI

Mercury in Gemini natives are quick-witted, curious, and intellectual. They are excellent communicators, writers, and teachers, and tend to be good at school. With varied interests, they seem to know a little about everything. They only have to take care to delve more deeply into subject matter. Because they are restless and absorb information quickly, they learn best in stimulating environments that move at a fast pace. Possessing logical minds, their intuition sometimes falls short. While they are skilled at conveying intellectual thoughts, they can be cold when communicating more personally. They might consider expressing more heart when speaking about emotional matters. However, they are generally smooth talkers—engaging and entertaining conversationalists, with brilliant senses of humor.

MERCURY IN CANCER

Mercury in Cancer natives are gentle, intuitive speakers. They can be wonderfully adept at communicating with the public, able to feel out an audience and adapt their speech to the energy of a room. Thoughtful and sensitive souls, their words are saturated with feeling. Learning subjectively, they respond more to personal stories than to cold hard facts. They are excellent listeners. While seemingly slow, they hear everything and retain it for a long time. Their voices tend to have melodic lulls that make people feel safe and protected. They are solid and sure-footed in their speech, in addition to being pleasant and soothing.

MERCURY IN LEO

Mercury in Leo natives are persuasive, dramatic, and authoritative speakers who possess a performative flair when conveying their thoughts. Their style of speech is convincing yet warm, and they tend to be infectiously idealistic and sure of their beliefs. They are typically drawn to creative subjects, and yearn to express themselves in artistic ways. While excellent communicators and leaders, it would serve them to develop more humility around their points of view, tempering their grandiosity. While they are quite ambitious, these natives love to play. They will generate much enthusiasm around any projects they enjoy. They are not built for tedious work and must find a way to direct their mental energies toward more imaginative and inspiring pursuits.

MERCURY IN VIRGO

Mercury in Virgo natives are excellent analyzers, researchers, and writers. They often thrive in school, unafraid of tedious mental work. Endowed with impeccable logic, they have clear, sharp, and organized minds. Detail-oriented and practical, they seldom use superfluous language, preferring to be economical and precise with their words. Because of this, they are excellent editors. Great with facts and figures, they can keep a balanced budget and make incredibly useful friends and coworkers. Though humble, they are also perfectionistic, holding back when they speak. They benefit from relaxing and expanding their minds, and thinking more broadly and poetically.

MERCURY IN LIBRA

Mercury in Libra natives have wonderful minds, which are both intellectual and poetic. They long for equilibrium, both in the world and in their immediate surroundings. Because of this, they tend to study subjects related either to justice or the arts. A halo of beauty surrounds their words, and they possess a knack for writing, as well as charming and melodic patterns of speech. Social and friendly, they work well in partnerships, sometimes needing another person to take the lead on projects. Avoiding arguments, they find the least offensive ways to express feedback, sometimes struggling with being direct. However, this placement also imbues them with incredibly fair minds. They take great pains to weigh the pros and cons of every decision. Persuasive and diplomatic, they can seduce people with charming language, speech, and ideas. Like Virgos, they can be perfectionistic, wanting every decision to be balanced, beautiful, and fair, which often leads to indecision. They must work to develop their initiative, and to make room for disagreements and mistakes.

MERCURY IN SCORPIO

Mercury in Scorpio natives have deep and probing minds. They often enjoy intimate conversations where they discuss intangibles, including feelings, the occult, and theoretical science. They love to investigate and possess an incredible ability to observe every detail. Longing to reach the heart of any matter, they will dive into ideas and exchanges with probing minds, carrying others into their depths. This can make for incredibly passionate, intense, and fascinating conversationalists who have uncanny abilities to see through people and figure out what makes them tick. They only have to be wary of becoming manipulative, resentful, or stubborn. If they orient their powerful minds toward worthy pursuits, these natives will be extremely effective and strategic, accomplishing anything they set their minds to.

MERCURY IN SAGITTARIUS

Mercury in Sagittarius natives have big minds that orient toward truth seeking. They can be inspiring speakers and teachers who carry others into their expansive mind-streams. They possess an infectious desire to learn, and will push the boundaries of comfort, both other people's and their own. As such, they often study religion, philosophy, and far-away cultures, interested in anything that will broaden their points of view. Blunt and enthusiastic in their speech, they sometimes struggle with listening. While generally open-minded, they only have to be wary of dogmatic thinking. They appreciate directness and genuineness, and lack patience for circuitous speech and manipulation. When they aren't expressing their passionate beliefs, they have bright and cheerful minds, laughing readily with friends and strangers.

MERCURY IN CAPRICORN

Mercury in Capricorn natives have methodical, rational, and steady minds. They accomplish tasks with ambition and patience. Sometimes serious-minded, they can go too far with compartmentalization and creating order. Possessing a slower approach toward mental tasks and learning, they need to take their time to break down information into smaller, more workable pieces. While it takes them longer than most to remember things, once they do, they will never forget them. Shrewd, with excellent judgment, they love to study more practical subjects, like business, building, or woodworking. They are drawn to the past and are often fond of history and antiques. They are also talented at anything that requires good timing, like music and comedy. They only have to work toward loosening their skepticism and finding more expressive and emotional ways of communicating. Their precision and carefulness can be powerful assets but also keep them from taking risks or sharing too much.

MERCURY IN AQUARIUS

Mercury in Aquarius natives have beautiful, inventive minds, with qualities of creative genius. They are broad thinkers who remain objective, and enjoy discussing fascinating topics like quantum physics, the nature of reality, or the future of humanity. They think outside the box, easily coming up with inventions and original perspectives. Possessing strong intuition, ideas can flash into their minds, seemingly out of the ether. Electronically gifted, these natives are often at the forefront of technology. Sometimes confrontational, they have to work toward tempering their tendency toward shock value as they sometimes enjoy saying things that make people uncomfortable. However, this is also their gift. They push people to squirm and expand their minds beyond complacency.

MERCURY IN PISCES

Mercury in Pisces natives are dreamy and abstract, expressing themselves in gentle and otherworldly manners. They often miss the pragmatic details, focusing instead on the intangible realm of moods, energies, and feelings. Their speech is soft and compassionate, and they are excellent listeners. With an aversion to cold facts, they prefer nuance and to read between the lines. There is much wisdom to glean from their approach, and they only have to work toward becoming more practical. They are often absent-minded and intellectually shy or lacking in confidence. However, they are extraordinarily artistic and visionary thinkers, and can help others to expand their minds beyond physical reality, into more spiritual, theoretical, and nebulous domains. They are naturally gifted meditators, and tend to be students of spirituality. Able to channel and dip into imagination and illusion, they also often study dance, photography, filmmaking, poetry, and music.

VENUS

LOVE, CREATIVITY, AND VALUES

Venus is the planet of creativity, femininity, love, and pleasure. The artist, lover, and, in some traditions, the goddess of peace, she brings beauty, harmony, and abundance to all that she touches. The placement of Venus in our chart indicates how we relate to aesthetics, relationships, and wealth. It is where we attract others, indicating our charm, style, and sociability. Ruling creativity and pleasure, Venus tells the story of how we express ourselves artistically, what we enjoy, and how we connect with partners and friends. If our sparkle and social graces are apparent, we know Venus is present.

What and who do we love? How do we behave at a party? What is our personal style? Who do we attract, and how do we seduce? These are the types of questions our Venus placement can answer.

With Venus in Gemini, a person would love witty banter and accumulate many friends; they would have light-hearted attitudes toward love and could seem fickle in choosing their partners. Venus in Cancer natives tend to be nurturing, insecure, and unconditionally loving in their relationships; their creative expression is emotional and personal, and they love to create cozy, beautiful homes. Venus in Scorpio produces a deep love nature, with overwhelming intensity and sexuality; attracting mystery and darkness, these natives are prone to secret affairs, or at least deep, private, and meaningful connections.

At her worst, Venus can slip from beauty into vanity, from magnetism into manipulation. All that Venus rules is important to being human—romance, pleasure, artistry. We must only be wary not to take her alluring superficiality too seriously. In her integrity, she introduces balance, spaciousness, and acceptance. She is generous and charming, helping us feel like we all belong.

The following section describes Venus in each of the signs, including how we love, who we attract, and how we express ourselves creatively and socially.

VENUS IN ARIES

Venus in Aries natives are enthusiastic about love and creativity. When their attractions are piqued, they can become impulsive and assertive. Seeing love as competition, they enjoy a good conquest. Outgoing, fun, and exciting, they thrive socially, though they can sometimes overwhelm shyer types. Unless other planets in their charts are more domestic, they can be reluctant to settle down and orient toward another's needs. Attracting wild, energetic, and even combative partners, their relationships sometimes fizzle out as quickly as they begin. Both in their relationships and creative endeavors, people with Venus in Aries would benefit from slowing down and thinking more long-term before leaping into decisions. Early marriages are common with this placement.

VENUS IN TAURUS

Venus in Taurus natives are easygoing and pleasant to be around. They take love seriously, and their particular style of charm is steady and sensual. Careful in determining if a partner is a safe choice, they won't leap headlong into affairs or friendships. These are generous lovers who enjoy touching and kissing for long periods, giving and receiving massages, and eating decadent food. They easily attract wealth and good fortune, often through family or marriage. Venus rules Taurus, so Venus is strong in this placement—the planet of beauty falling in the sign of earthly pleasure. This means that these natives are likely to possess artistic talent, often becoming gifted chefs, dancers, ceramicists, or gardeners. They only have to be careful not to overindulge on food, wine, or pleasure of any kind.

VENUS IN GEMINI

Venus in Gemini natives are social butterflies and flirts, attracting people through their words and intellect. They begin love affairs and friendships first and foremost through the mind. With many interests and an ability to connect with a broad range of people, they can find it difficult to settle on one person or to make love the focus of their lives. Change, excitement, and mental stimulation are vital for their relationships to last. They channel their creativity into communication, writing, travel, and socializing. Naturally witty and charming, these natives find pleasure in having a variety of friends and many social gatherings to attend.

VENUS IN CANCER

Venus in Cancer natives are romantic, nurturing partners with tender hearts and the tendency to feel hurt and insecure in love. Reassuring, demonstrative partners who clearly express their feelings are essential for these vulnerable souls. Because of their watery and emotional love nature, stability is important in establishing friendships and romantic relationships. Feeling safe, they won't retreat into their shells, pincers out and moods thrashing. Within secure relationships, they are traditional, loyal, and devoted. These are the partners who will cook you dinner, love their children effusively and unconditionally, and remember the day that you met and exactly what you were wearing. Their creative work is personal and sentimental, and they do well having artistic outlets for their emotions. Creating a comfortable home is also helpful for these sensitive homebodies.

VENUS IN LEO

Venus in Leo natives are gregarious and warm, attracting people with their undeniable charisma, magnetism, and light. Loyal and generous, these are doting souls who will speak lovingly of their partners and friends, making them feel accepted and special. Wildly popular, they are the life of the party, entertaining people with their playfulness and extravagance. Often financially indulgent, these natives are the most likely to possess luxurious belongings and to spend their money decadently. They need to have fun and express themselves creatively and boisterously. They are often endowed with significant creative talents and the ability to perform. They only have to curb their dramatic nature, as well as their great need to be admired and adored.

VENUS IN VIRGO

Venus in Virgo natives are loyal and devoted to their friends and partners. They will work hard to be of service to those they love, readily helping with menial tasks, like moving, bringing food to sick friends, or helping to edit a proposal. Often they are talented writers—witty and refined. Reticent in love, they are like cats, taking their time to open to new partners. Once they do, they are warm, affectionate, and even doting. They only have to be careful not to dissect and criticize their partners and loved ones too much. This is part of their self-protection, as they fear being hurt or opening to partners who are unworthy. Their discernment also lends to refined sensibilities, but when directed toward people, it can go too far. Around finances, they are careful, restrained, and shrewd.

VENUS IN LIBRA

Venus in Libra natives are in love with love. They easily fall for people, seeing the best in everyone and giving them the space to be exactly who they are. Perceptive in matters of the heart and aesthetics, they can easily harmonize the energies of a room and other people. Venus rules Libra, so this placement is strong. This is the most romantic placement of the zodiac, generating charm, flirtatiousness, and sensitivity to beauty. Responsive to poetry, candlelight, and other such gestures, these natives are prone to seduction by way of sweet nothings. On the other hand, they are also seductive, persuasive, and charming themselves. Finding the right words, scents, and outfits to draw people in, they easily land the object of their desires. Talented in the realms of design, fashion, writing, and the more intellectual arts, these natives do well when making use of their creative gifts. They are able to manifest their dreams and magnetize abundance. However, they also adore luxury and can spend extravagantly. Accommodating souls who are quite attached to others, these natives thrive in all kinds of partnerships, romantic and otherwise.

VENUS IN SCORPIO

Venus in Scorpio natives are intense and passionate lovers, who sometimes teeter into obsession. Sexual magnetism is strong with this placement, and they tend to lead with intimacy, total commitment, and complete focus on whomever they meet. Love is all-encompassing for them—an almost spiritual experience. They want to possess their partner and make them fully surrender, physically and psychologically. It would help them to let go more, to avoid secret affairs, and to release their vindictive tendencies when things don't go their way. They would also do well directing their energies toward their powerful artistic natures and healthier plunges into emotional connection. When balanced, these natives are capable of profound healing, transformative love, and transcendent creative expression.

VENUS IN SAGITTARIUS

Venus in Sagittarius natives are fun to have around. Desirable friends, they are friendly, humorous, cheerful, and sociable. They possess adventurous love natures, enjoying connections with a broad variety of people, making them hard to pin down. Friendships are often easier than relationships for these natives, and they do best with partners who are primarily friends and adventure buddies. They need someone who can keep the affair exciting and who shares similar beliefs and values. These natives require freedom to be themselves fully, and to expand their horizons continuously. Good fortune comes to them when they travel to faraway lands, and they often end up with partners from foreign countries and with different cultural backgrounds. They strive toward perfection in love, which could feel just out of reach. They would do well working with their fear of being possessed while also releasing unrealistic ideals.

VENUS IN CAPRICORN

Venus in Capricorn natives are traditional lovers who desire commitment and usually marriage. Serious and reserved, they can sometimes hold back in expressing their romantic feelings. They tend to fear loneliness and rejection, seldom taking big risks when it comes to love. Steadfast and loyal, they are dependable friends, partners, and parents. They only have to be careful not to repress their feelings of dependency and desire, or to go cold when they feel snubbed. Working through issues of control could help thaw their romantic natures, allowing them to open more to emotional connection and genuine social exchanges. They can be talented musicians and dancers, since their creative expression is imbued with a brilliant sense of timing. Supportive of others' ambitions, they can be wonderfully helpful in assisting their loved ones as they work toward achieving their goals.

VENUS IN AQUARIUS

Venus in Aquarius natives can be unconventional in their love natures, pushing the boundaries of social convention and determining their own rules in their relationships. This doesn't mean they aren't willing to commit. They just like to be the ones to decide what makes sense for them in partnerships, rather than adhering to preordained rules. Experimental and electrically magnetic, these natives fall in love in sudden bursts that can just as suddenly go cold. They desire absolute freedom in love to be themselves and express their uniqueness. They are wonderful at bringing together groups of friends and communities. Their love for humanity is often easier to access than their love within intimate relationships. Accordingly, they tend to orient their creativity and passion toward helping the less fortunate. Highly intuitive and inventive, they generate original ideas, electrifying whoever is around them. If harnessed properly, they have incredible powers of manifestation, which could help to shape the future, bringing benefit to many others.

VENUS IN PISCES

Venus in Pisces natives are highly sensitive and gentle in love. Romantic, dreamy, and self-sacrificing, they can merge fully with partners and friends. These souls demonstrate the highest form of love—unconditional, transcendent, and non-judgmental. They are extremely compassionate and possess a deep need to feel understood. Love can feel confusing for them, as they are prone to changing with the tides of whomever they are with. Because their empathy is so strong, they tend to attract downtrodden and needy people, who might take advantage of their kindness. It would help them to temper their martyrdom and establish healthier boundaries around their relationships and friendships. These souls are often gifted in the realms of art, music, and poetry. They at least feel these things deeply, with great appreciation. Highly sensitive to nature, they are able to connect with the magic of the earth, and especially the ocean, feeling replenished by their beauty.

MARS
PHYSICAL EXERTION, INITIATIVE, AND SEXUALITY

God of war, Mars is a masculine planet, embodying our physical energy, style of aggression, and sexuality. The placement of our Mars indicates our drive and temperament. It shows what captures us at first sight, and who sparks our animal attractions.

What are our passions? Are we courageous or timid? What and who do we pursue? How do we behave when we are aroused or angry? These are the types of questions our Mars sign begins to answer.

For example, Mars in Leo natives are impulsive and prone to dramatic affairs; even with the rest of their planets falling in shyer signs, these natives will express confidence and playfulness sexually, in competition, or onstage. People with Mars in Taurus are driven to create material security, and often possess stubbornness and tenacity once they initiate a project; they are sensual lovers and dancers, slowly relishing the body and touch. Those with Mars in Libra have artistic drives, but sometimes waver before initiating projects or affairs; they are attracted to classically beautiful partners and can sometimes lose themselves to languid days, requiring a push to leap into action or express their anger.

At its worst, Mars can easily flip from drive and determination to aggression and insensitivity. If we're feeling quick-tempered and hostile, we know Mars is present. At its best, Mars can show up valiantly, with courage and ample energy to take action and complete a task. It is our bravery and virility, which helps us take risks and move ahead.

The following section describes Mars in each of the signs, including our drive, temperament, attractions, and sexual nature.

MARS IN ARIES

Mars in Aries natives are enthusiastic souls with high energy and the gift of knowing exactly what they want. They will pursue their interests without hesitation, drawing on their inner store of courage and assertiveness. Sexually, they won't prolong their seduction or foreplay. They are direct and cut to the chase, eagerly going after what they want. Their physical prowess and exertion are unparalleled, and they have the potential to be impressive athletes. They only have to be wary of becoming domineering or tactless, tending to act as soon as they feel an impulse. Fiery and impetuous, they can be quick to anger and arousal—and they can just as quickly change their minds. Humility, restraint, and mindfulness would be helpful to develop, in order to avoid unnecessary confrontation and heartache.

MARS IN TAURUS

Mars in Taurus natives are able to pace themselves, directing their steady energy toward creating beauty and material security. Practical, determined, and stubborn, it would be hard to deter them from attaining their desires in any aspect of life. They are gifted manifesters, able to materialize their dreams, which often involve luxury and sensual pleasure. Sexual beings, they orient strongly toward relationships, and can sometimes become overly possessive of their lovers. They are attracted to classical beauty and strength, and they are often physically fit themselves. Uncomplicated and direct in their approach to love-making, they take their time to feel each moment with slow intensity. They must only avoid becoming too dogged or stubborn in their arguments. Holding their emotions too tightly, they have the potential to erupt into anger and resentment.

MARS IN GEMINI

Mars in Gemini natives exert themselves primarily toward matters of the mind. They pride themselves in their wit and gift of debate, and quite enjoy intellectual contests and sparring. Sexually, their entry point is through words and conversation, finding flirtation to be deeply arousing. With varied interests and attractions, they sometimes have many affairs and changes in direction. After all, they are easily stimulated with their insatiable curiosities. They make for compelling writers, teachers, and speakers, and can lead and command others with their powerful minds. It would be helpful for these natives to develop athletic routines to avoid becoming caught in their heads. Too much thinking can generate anxiety and impede forward momentum. It would also help to deepen their connections and commitments, rather than jumping around with incurable restlessness.

MARS IN CANCER

Mars in Cancer natives lead with their deeply sensitive and emotional drives. Their persuasiveness is gently overpowering, as they easily influence others, adjusting to whatever energies are in front of them. In lovemaking, they can be quite gifted—profoundly intuitive, nurturing, and skillful. However, they require their partners to be receptive or they will shut down. Sensitive to their surroundings, they can explode with irritability, their anger releasing in moody waves. Prone to codependency, they find it difficult to let go of lovers—even when the relationship is clearly over. They thrive when engaged in emotional work. This provides them with healthy outlets for their ample sensitivity and perceptiveness.

MARS IN LEO

Mars in Leo natives are magnetic and sometimes dramatic souls. Sexually impulsive and direct, they are playful, loyal, and affectionate lovers, who require ample attention. In return, they lavish their partners with warmth and praise. Quite visionary, they can achieve grand goals. They are often drawn to creative pursuits, and enjoy having outlets where they can perform and express themselves artistically. While fun to be around, they must be wary of becoming too volatile, self-centered, and domineering. However, they are self-sufficient and make for excellent leaders, as long as they can keep their egos intact. Attracted to performers and artists, they are easily aroused by partners who are popular and receive a lot of attention themselves. Their exaggerated passions and theatrics sometimes lead them to jealousy and overreactions.

MARS IN VIRGO

Mars in Virgo natives are hard workers and careful planners who devote themselves to projects and people with integrity, loyalty, and attention to detail. Their energies are primarily practical and useful, and they make excellent doctors, nurses, and social workers. They orient toward health and are always ready to be of service to others. They keep their sexuality under wraps, but once they become intimate with their partner, they are warm and passionate. Their trust has to be earned in order to open up. Drawn to intelligent, pure, and put-together people, their ideal mate is the person next door. Detail-oriented and persistent, they are able to harness their sensible minds to accomplish their goals. They only have to be wary of becoming stuck in the hamster wheel of perfectionism. Physical activities could help them let go of nervous tension and the need to control. Meditation and developing their imagination would also help them find balance and orient toward the bigger picture.

MARS IN LIBRA

Mars in Libra natives may find that the high energy and anger of this virile planet is hampered by a preoccupation with social rules, fairness, and an intense need for approval. The energy of this placement is primarily artistic and intellectual, and natives must work to express their physical energies. They are drawn to beauty, typically choosing refined and classically attractive mates. Vulgarity is a turn-off, and they feel aroused in luxurious and refined settings. They move gracefully and tend to be aesthetically driven. While they possess a strong impetus toward relationships, they will not play the role of initiator, preferring instead to be pursued. When the planet of aggression falls into the sign of diplomacy, natives can easily become indecisive and lazy. They will carefully consider both sides before making a move, which can impede their ability to be decisive. Because they can see every angle, they make for excellent litigators and mediators. They only have to work on their ability to face aggression and confrontation, which can be helpful in shaking them out of complacency and stagnation.

MARS IN SCORPIO

Mars in Scorpio natives are strong-willed, self-reliant, and highly disciplined, with spades of emotional, physical, and intellectual energy.

If they decide to do something, nothing will stand in their way. Drawn to danger, mystery, and intensity, they have a powerful drive that propels them toward emotionally charged people and situations. They will face anything they choose to with obsessive determination. With deep sexual natures, they are exploratory and sometimes dark. Prone to jealousy, controlling behavior, and resentment, they can demonstrate explosive temperaments when slighted. With powerful magnetism, they would do well working with the public. Their ample imagination and creativity could lead them to becoming talented artists, musicians, or performers. Always investigating and probing beneath the surface, they could also become gifted therapists, scientists, or healers.

MARS IN SAGITTARIUS

Sagittarius is the most athletic and enthusiastic placement for Mars, though natives can sometimes lack in practicality. They are drawn to travel and adventure, at times becoming reckless and impulsive—pushing the limits of danger for the sake of excitement and learning. They will fight for their beliefs, courageously defending their philosophical convictions. However, they are also resoundingly cheerful, inspiring others with optimism and expansiveness. Enjoying sexual exploration, they like to experience many conquests, especially in young adulthood. They are attracted to partners who come from different countries and ideological backgrounds, finding stimulation in broadening their horizons through differentness and novelty. They are drawn to spirituality and do well with body-wisdom practices, such as yoga, tai chi, or qigong. In order to stay in a relationship, they will need ample freedom, joy, adventure, and sexual variation.

MARS IN CAPRICORN

Mars in Capricorn natives are deliberate and steady in accomplishing their goals, though they sometimes lack in emotional energy. Because they exhibit incredible restraint, they are able to accomplish a lot, striving carefully toward career ambitions and recognition. They only have to avoid becoming workaholics or overly cautious. Taking risks, seeking pleasure, and breaking out of old patterns could help them to expand their opportunities in all facets of life. Learning that emotional expression can exist alongside dignity and respectability could help these natives to relax their public demeanors, which are sometimes too stiff. With strong sexual drives, they are known to retain virility into old age, often relaxing their self-control later in life. Mostly traditional about sex, they approach it with commitment and integrity. They are attracted to mates who are proper, successful, and mature, and can be wonderfully powerful, long-lasting, rhythmic lovers. Possessing excellent timing, they could also become talented comedians and musicians.

MARS IN AQUARIUS

Mars in Aquarius natives are drawn to the realm of ideas, exerting their energy toward progressive and intellectual endeavors. They push boundaries and are not afraid to argue their points with creative, eccentric, and distinctive styles. Stubborn and nontraditional, they will seldom give in to opposing points of view, especially if they are unoriginal. Attracted to all things and people living outside the box, they yearn for novelty, aroused by rebellious souls and nonconformity. Sexually, they will make their own rules and enjoy having the freedom to bend the constraints of what's considered normal and acceptable.

When they've found a mate whose mind and perspective they respect, they can become much more stable partners, relaxing their obstinacy and impatience.

MARS IN PISCES

Mars in Pisces natives exert their energy primarily toward fantasy and emotion, sometimes lacking in practicality and physical energy. This placement often falls in the charts of artists, musicians, poets, and other creative types, where this potential is best manifested. Sensitive souls, they require much time alone to reflect and regenerate. They are drawn to partners who are gentle, spiritual, and compassionate, and often find love at first sight in artists who are able to capture their hearts and imaginations. They can merge completely with their partners, finding the act of sex to be spiritual and all-encompassing. Receptive and highly romantic, these natives only have to be sure that they've set clear boundaries and that they've firmly established their intentions. Otherwise, they risk becoming resentful and withdrawn as they lose themselves in other people.

6

THE SOCIAL PLANETS

Jupiter and Saturn

J UPITER AND SATURN are known as the social planets. Less personal than the inner planets, they represent how we relate to the world at large. Saturn rules government, traditions, and society, representing contraction and limitation, while Jupiter rules religion, philosophy, and humor, representing expansion and limitless possibilities.

The ruler of gravity, Saturn forces us to root to the earth while imposing restraint, responsibility, and hard lessons. He teaches us to mature and participate in society so we can become accountable for people other than ourselves. An opposite energy to Saturn, Jupiter inspires joy, adventure, travel, and optimism. He orients us toward philosophy and spirituality through shared belief systems. Both of these planets hold keys for us to access the esoteric wisdom of the outer planets, with Saturn as the ultimate gatekeeper. First, we must look to the horizon in pursuit of wisdom (Jupiter), then ground and take care of ourselves (Saturn) before delving into the lessons of the more complex outer planets.

Since Jupiter and Saturn move slowly, their sign placements reveal less about our individual nature than our Sun, Moon, Ascendant, and inner planets. As they orbit the Sun from the position of Earth, Jupiter remains in one sign for a year, while Saturn stays for two and a half years. (By comparison, the Sun moves through a sign every month; the Moon every two and a half days.)

JUPITER
GOOD FORTUNE, EXPANSION, AND ABUNDANCE

Jupiter is the most joyful planet, representing humor, abundance, expansion, and good fortune. It tells us where we have luck, what comes easily to us, and where doors are likely to open for us. The Romans honored the god Jupiter more than any other. He was considered the god of sky, who granted auspiciousness and symbolized faith and wisdom. In astrology, the planet Jupiter represents similar qualities, showing us how we orient toward religion, ideology, prosperity, and higher education.

The largest planet in our solar system, Jupiter not only speaks to our luck and expansion, it also tells the story of how we relate to some weightier facets of life. Our Jupiter sign answers questions like: How tolerant are we? What do we believe in? Where do we show up as irresponsible, extreme, or blindly optimistic?

For example, people with Jupiter in Libra could find great success through artistic endeavors, teamwork, and relationships; they could go too far emphasizing romance, even becoming love addicts. Jupiter in Capricorn natives demonstrate ample discipline, strong family lives, and hard work; they could become successful politicians or public servants, and must only be wary of their tendency toward closed-mindedness. Jupiter in Aquarius natives display extreme tolerance and originality, often becoming inventors, philanthropists, and humanitarians; financially irresponsible, they must work consciously toward establishing stability, which could balance their gifts.

The following section describes Jupiter in each sign, including our philosophies, how we find expansion, luck, and success, and where we go too far.

JUPITER IN ARIES

Those with Jupiter in Aries have innate leadership abilities. Enthusiastic students and teachers, they are often pioneers in the realms of philosophy, religion, and higher education. Confident and independent, they place much of their energy toward self-improvement. These natives are often successful in entrepreneurialism, magnetizing great fortune becoming their own boss. Often lucky in their youth, they must avoid becoming too careless or impulsive around money and business. Developing practicality and restraint would help to balance their gifts.

JUPITER IN TAURUS

People with Jupiter in Taurus are often lucky around money and resources, easily establishing financial stability and abundance. With large appetites, they are fond of luxury, prioritizing good food, beautiful surroundings, and maintaining the best lifestyle they can afford. With the gift of manifestation, these natives easily attract what they need or desire. Conservative in their views, they establish security and safety in their lives, exerting patience and determination toward business pursuits. They must only avoid becoming too rigid in their beliefs.

JUPITER IN GEMINI

Those with Jupiter in Gemini have open minds and expansive curiosities. Abundant friendships, conversations, and travel bring good fortune to these natives. With diverse interests, they sometimes struggle to become experts on a single subject, fluently bouncing from one idea to the next. Known for their intellect and communication abilities, they can become influential teachers, writers, speakers, and politicians. While lively, fun, and interesting people, they are restless souls. With increased focus, they could transform their ample knowledge into mastery and deeper wisdom.

JUPITER IN CANCER

Those with Jupiter in Cancer have strong moral backbones, likely instilled by their parents in early childhood. Generous in spirit, these souls are kind, tender, and bright. They are innate nurturers, willing to support anyone who is struggling. They generate joy and emotional abundance by creating stable home lives, feeding their inner worlds, and taking care of family and friends. They succeed when they have strong connections with their mothers, or have at least worked on healing their parental wounds. Because security is important to these natives, they are usually frugal and eventually become wealthy as a result. They can overindulge on food and must work to avoid health problems from emotional overeating.

JUPITER IN LEO

Jupiter in Leo natives are highly expansive, easily demonstrating their confidence and optimism. Believing in the power of benevolence and generosity, they happily share any wealth they acquire. With abundant physical and emotional strength, they make charismatic leaders. Dignity comes easily to these regal souls, who can inspire people to live their joy, seek pleasure, and express their talents to the world. Developing humility would help to balance their gifts, as they sometimes teeter into egotism. Coming from pure intention, their expansive hearts and assertiveness can help create much good in the world as they lead others with drama, humor, and cheerful grandeur. It would be wise for these natives to avoid their tendency to gamble.

JUPITER IN VIRGO

Those with Jupiter in Virgo attract abundance and good fortune when engaging their gifts of practicality, hard work, and attention to detail. They feel most expansive when serving the greater good and devoting themselves to others. These souls are not risk takers. Instead, pragmatism and careful planning help them to attract what they desire. They need clear goals and discernible outcomes, and must be careful not to limit their vision of what's possible. Surrendering their caution and opening to magic could help to expand their sometimes cynical and overly scientific perspectives. Spirituality and meditation could balance their gifts and help to assuage excessive worrying.

JUPITER IN LIBRA

Jupiter in Libra natives exhibit significant charm, diplomacy, and creativity. Through relationships, strategic friendships, and marriage, they can attract wealth and expansion. Teamwork and partnerships are keys to their success, and they especially benefit from connecting with people who share similar principles. With a strong understanding of justice and fairness, they often become effective peacemakers, mediators, and lawyers. Their ample artistic potential could lead them to becoming successful designers, musicians, and visual artists. They easily resonate with the spiritual side of beauty and creative expression. Highly persuasive, these natives are influential people, shaping society with balanced and attractive ideologies. They must only be wary of placing too much emphasis on relationships. Developing independence, assertion, and confidence will help to balance their many gifts.

JUPITER IN SCORPIO

People with Jupiter in Scorpio exude tremendous personal power, magnetizing others with an aura of fascination and intrigue. They have the ability to affect people deeply and emotionally, and can make excellent therapists, healers, musicians, and politicians. They have the ability to shine light on whatever is hidden—exposing secrets, delving into research, and solving mysteries. Sexual relationships can bring luck and expansion to these natives, who benefit most of all from members of the opposite sex. With luck around money and inheritance, they can become quite wealthy if their Jupiter forms helpful angles with other planets (see chapter 8). Determination and willpower are strong with this placement, as natives hold tight to unflappable ideologies. They must be wary of imposing their beliefs onto others or becoming too fixated on sex and power. Good fortune comes when they master the art of letting go.

JUPITER IN SAGITTARIUS

Jupiter in Sagittarius natives are big-minded and optimistic individuals. This is the most fortunate placement of Jupiter because here it falls in its natural sign. Generous and carefree, these natives can be inspiring individuals who lead others in adventure, athletics, and intellectual or spiritual pursuits. Expansion comes when they immerse themselves in nature, philosophy, religion, and meditation. With strong convictions, they can be wonderful teachers, professors, and lecturers, and must only be wary of becoming too dogmatic. Money is easy for them to magnetize, but they could also become big spenders, unable to retain their wealth. It would benefit them to develop restraint and pragmatism. However, their buoyancy and zeal are also their gifts, helping them to lead exciting lives, experiencing joy and humor as they accomplish their lofty goals.

JUPITER IN CAPRICORN

Those with Jupiter in Capricorn can be wonderfully successful. Good fortune comes when they focus their energies on helping society, starting families, and respecting tradition. With an abundant sense of mores and ethics, these natives often assume large responsibilities in life, holding political offices or running large companies. They have the potential to be quite powerful, as they possess a strong sense of duty as well as tremendous ambition. They only have to be wary of becoming too conservative and rigid. Opening their minds to innovation while orienting toward the future could help to balance their gifts.

JUPITER IN AQUARIUS

Jupiter in Aquarius natives are wonderfully tolerant and accepting people who value others' differences. With progressive outlooks, these souls could help to advance society. Great fortune comes when they are engaged in humanitarian and technological pursuits, and when they orient toward creating the future. Revolutionaries and renegades, these souls can make great strides in inventive and creative fields, bringing communities together, and coming up with original concepts. They sometimes lack in financial resources because they are not very concerned with material wealth. Developing their sense of responsibility and security could help to balance their considerable gifts.

JUPITER IN PISCES

Jupiter in Pisces natives are often mystics and spiritualists, with enormous compassion for the less fortunate. They experience great expansion when focused on the spiritual or artistic sides of life. Because of their broad empathy, they would do well in professions where they work directly with people, or where they can productively engage their emotionality and sensitivity. Able to relate to anyone, they attract success through their immense likability. However, they often prefer solitude and working behind the scenes. Alone time can bring good fortune, as well as meditation and focusing on the inner, spiritual side of life. They only have to make sure they stay rooted to the earth, developing practical wisdom and taking good care of their bodies and health.

SATURN
RESPONSIBILITY, RESTRAINT, AND AMBITION

Saturn is the planet of obstacles, responsibility, and ambition. It forces us to mature by presenting us with adversity. By holding up mirrors, we must face ourselves honestly, developing awareness around what to accept and what to reject. Where are we making the same mistakes again and again? Where do we resist growing into dependable adults? With Saturn's conscious awareness, we can begin to show up more dutifully for our families, careers, and society.

Saturn proves that the places where we struggle are also our gifts. As we make efforts toward overcoming our weaknesses, they become our strengths. Without Saturn, we might be complacent souls who only seek instant gratification. Saturn grounds us to the earth and to each other, encouraging us to develop trustworthiness and proficiency. Ruling time and constraints, Saturn bestows us with longevity and durability, helping us to attain our long-term goals. The sign our Saturn falls into reveals our challenges, where we work hard, and how we attain mastery.

For example, while Saturn in Virgo natives are practical, highly intelligent, and hardworking, they can become stifled by their excessive attention to detail; self-critical and subservient, they must work to broaden their scopes and realize their value and potential. Those with Saturn in Sagittarius take their spirituality and ideologies seriously;

they could become religious authorities or professors of philosophy, and must work to let go of rigid beliefs. People with Saturn in Pisces can create meaningful careers around their imaginations, but material success could be hard to attain; compassionate souls, they must work to avoid self-sacrificing and recognize that prioritizing their personal expression is what helps others the most.

The following section describes Saturn in each sign, including our obstacles, discipline, morality, and how we can achieve long-term success.

SATURN IN ARIES

Those with Saturn in Aries could find their energies and drive stifled in early life. They are often given ample responsibilities as young people, which hampers their innocence and ambition. They must work hard at developing their confidence and assertiveness so they can express themselves more fully. Otherwise, their repressed passions could lead them to feeling excessive anger. Even still, outsiders will see them as people who are very much in control, marked by their self-sufficiency and restraint. However, these natives may also seem weak or grumpy as they face tremendous obstacles in life. Later on, they could become quite powerful as they work through their challenges around initiative and leadership. Sometimes, they even become extreme risk takers to make up for their hampered courage and strength. They experience significantly less difficulties as they grow older.

SATURN IN TAURUS

Saturn in Taurus natives place tremendous emphasis on attaining financial and romantic security. They have exaggerated fears around not having enough, and can develop excessive prudence as a result.

Early in life, they may find it difficult to establish wealth and love. They will work hard to save as much as possible and remain committed to their partners, even in toxic relationships. Patient and disciplined, they eventually find success, usually in older age. When it does happen, these natives are generous and continue to demonstrate powerful determination. At this point, they could help others in need, since they understand what it means to struggle. They are also capable of becoming successful in artistic careers, applying their discipline toward mastering their art.

SATURN IN GEMINI

Saturn in Gemini natives have strong mental abilities, with excellent logic, rationality, and adaptability. Gifted mathematicians and scientists, they are able to apply their disciplined minds toward systematically solving problems and studying for long periods of time. Difficulties with communication or public speaking could arise, as well as obtaining education as young people. However, what they do learn they will never forget as they are able to blend Gemini's wit and intellect with the mastery and pragmatism of Saturn. This helps them to deepen and retain their studies. Economical with their words, they can become powerful speakers later in life. They can also apply their intelligence and common sense toward business pursuits, often attaining tremendous success.

SATURN IN CANCER

Saturn in Cancer natives can be emotionally repressive, obscuring their true feelings in order to protect themselves. Family can become a source of struggle for them, as they feel weighed down by familial duty, and unable to access genuine connection. These natives must work hard toward unlocking their emotional expression, otherwise they risk becoming depressed and unable to establish intimacy. In balance, they can translate their sensitivity into business savvy and become quite successful, building careers that are close to their hearts. Relaxing their shells and mastering their emotional natures are key for these natives. With effort, they have the potential to become quite emotionally adept, devoting themselves wholeheartedly to family and nurturing others. They only have to commit to doing their inner work, thus opening to the deep lessons available to them.

SATURN IN LEO

Those with Saturn in Leo place great emphasis on the need for recognition. They long to be in charge, which leads them to becoming overly dictatorial. While the potential for warmth is somewhat stifled by this combination, these natives have strong wills and the ability to assume great responsibility. Pleasure and creativity can be hard to come by with this placement. Joy, humor, and artistic expression loom beneath the surface, while they yearn to have an audience and vehicle for their creative gifts. These challenges could cause them pain and turmoil. As parents, they can be strict with their children, feeling overly burdened by parenthood. If they work on establishing healthy confidence, their self-image will improve, along with their relationships with others. Later in life, they are better able to relax, have fun, and connect with joy and exuberance. This becomes especially true as they begin to develop mastery around creative expression.

SATURN IN VIRGO

Saturn in Virgo natives can place tremendous emphasis on perfectionism and attention to detail. Overly cautious, they could find it difficult to step back and see the bigger picture. They excel in research, strategizing, and data management, and could become quite successful through careful planning and prudent investments. Sometimes these natives struggle with health. As they work to heal themselves, they could become great masters of medicine, herbalism, or nutrition. If they can release their pessimism, they are able to work hard in service of others, with a strong sense of morality. They can become successful in menial work, and will find helpful and practical ways of distributing their wealth to others. Conscientious, devoted, and intelligent, these hard workers will easily achieve their goals and will do so humbly and selflessly. The key to their success is to curb their excessive self-criticism.

SATURN IN LIBRA

Saturn in Libra natives are fair-minded, with deep longing to create a just and balanced society. They could become known for their artistic abilities and magnetism, as they are able to control their charm and persuasiveness and use it to their advantage. They often experience setbacks around relationships and marriage, and could divorce early or find a steady partner later in life. Hard work in love could reap big rewards for these natives, who could become masters in establishing balanced, healthy relationships with patience and persistence. Socializing could feel like work, but this placement also denotes an ability to win friends, which could lead to success in their careers.

SATURN IN SCORPIO

Those with Saturn in Scorpio have tremendous personal power, which comes from their subtlety and deep emotional understanding. They have the capacity to be quite controlling and manipulative if they are not working from pure intention. They hide their intensity with friendlier exteriors, seldom betraying their messier emotions. Calculating and determined, they can become successful in any endeavor. They are sometimes the center of scandals or gossip, or endure the death of a loved one early in life. However, these difficulties make them stronger and wiser, and they have the capacity to go far with their self-mastery through their adversities. If they work hard at looking at themselves honestly, they will be able to glimpse the nature of reality firsthand, and will be able to become powerful spiritual teachers or healers.

SATURN IN SAGITTARIUS

Saturn in Sagittarius natives place much emphasis on religion, philosophy, and higher education. They often become experts in these subjects, establishing careers as religious leaders, philosophers, writers, or professors. This placement often requires natives to master patience, and success could feel thwarted until later in life. Facing adversities, they can develop tremendous wisdom, which they then impart to others. Sometimes tension exists between their desire for freedom and stability. Engaging in disciplined work that requires travel, studying foreign cultures, and athleticism could help to merge these opposing needs. Obstacles might arise around higher education, but with perseverance these natives could end up earning many degrees. They must only be wary of fundamentalism, as their belief systems could easily become too fixed.

SATURN IN CAPRICORN

Saturn in Capricorn natives are ambitious, traditional, and persevering. In its natural sign, Saturn here emphasizes the importance of integrity in their families and careers. Highly pragmatic, those with Saturn in Capricorn are natural businesspeople, politicians, and leaders. Slow and steady, they will make their way to the pinnacle of success with unflappable determination. Obstacles often arise in youth, but they only strengthen the resilience of these natives. They often end up in positions of authority later in life, having overcome hardships while earning the respect of others. Depression and melancholy are possible, as are good senses of humor. Saturn rules time, and these natives have great timing, making then skilled comedians and musicians. They only have to be wary of suppressive conservatism. They would benefit from opening their minds to innovation and inclusion.

SATURN IN AQUARIUS

Saturn in Aquarius natives have great ideas around how to create enlightened society. Blending the pragmatism and systemization of Saturn with the innovation and originality of Aquarius, they can come up with practical, yet novel ideas around solving societal problems. Often funny, stubborn, and clever souls, they can be iconoclasts who isolate themselves inadvertently as they struggle to belong. However, they can be quite popular in the public sphere, becoming known as either politicians or entertainers, catching people off guard with their creative genius and progressive yet solid ideologies. Democratic and scientific, their cool logic will take them very far if they can be sure to work from their hearts, avoiding the trap of hyperconservatism or pessimism.

SATURN IN PISCES

Saturn in Pisces natives could become quite serious about spiritual pursuits. They have powerful imaginations and deep compassion. However, attaining material success could be challenging. Becoming skillful meditators, spiritual teachers, filmmakers, or artists would make good use of their potentials. They only have to avoid self-sacrifice, understanding that they will help others most if they develop their immense personal gifts. Sensitive souls, these natives might experience significant loss in their lives. Their hard lessons will culminate when they can surrender and then direct their focus on merging their spirituality with society in pragmatic ways, skillfully joining heaven and earth. Meditation, time alone and in nature, and studying dreams and the unconscious could help to unlock their innate talents.

7

THE OUTER PLANETS

Uranus, Neptune, and Pluto

JUST BEYOND the social planets, we reach the outer planets—Uranus, Neptune, and Pluto. These planets are so far away from Earth, they are invisible to the human eye. They represent the most esoteric aspects of ourselves—the invisible qualities of life that push us outside our comfort zone and into the sublime. Uranus rules intuition and the future; Neptune rules healing and spirituality; and Pluto is power and transformation. In other terms, Uranus is the occultist, Neptune is the mystic, and Pluto the shaman. They are all magical in different ways, bringing us depth and dimensionality.

Because they are so remote, the outer planets move significantly slower than the others. Uranus takes 84 years to move through the zodiac; Neptune takes 164 years, and Pluto 248. This means the signs of the outer planets describe whole generations rather than individual traits. They affect us personally as well, but this is determined by the houses they fall into and the aspects they form to our personal planets or significant points in our chart (covered in chapters 8 and 9).

In the meantime, we can begin to relate to these important energies by learning the meaning of the outer planets in each sign. We can see how we resonate with the energies of our own placements, and how they apply to the broader scope of our generations and peer groups.

URANUS
INTUITION, REBELLION, AND REVOLUTION

Uranus is the planet of intuition, electricity, and revolution. When connecting to Uranus, our intuition strikes like lightning, opening our minds to cosmic portals. Innovation, creative genius, and flashes of insight are all signs that Uranus is in effect. It is the great awakener, who jolts us out of complacency, sometimes through sudden change and chaos. Considered a higher octave of Mercury, which rules the intellectual mind, Uranus will take our ordinary perceptions and add crystalline dimensions. If Mercury is science, Uranus is theoretical physics.

Uranus pushes boundaries and rebels without second-guessing. It drives us forward by bucking the status quo and inciting revolution. Rules and traditions mean nothing to this rebellious planet, which requires absolute authenticity. Deeply humanitarian, Uranus embodies the potential for creating enlightened society, and upholding values of open-mindedness and acceptance. Also ruling technology and the future, Uranus will lead us to inventions that expand human possibility, finding solutions to the world's problems.

Since Saturn is the gatekeeper to the higher realms, how much we can access the power of Uranus depends on how far we've gone with Saturn's lessons. If we've mastered discipline and pragmatism and faced ourselves honestly, we can walk through the gates of Uranus, and beyond. We can begin to experiment and push the boundaries of existing paradigms. It is like the violinist, painter, or poet who has mastered the rules of their art, and now they can begin breaking them, creating their own patterns and compositions.

The following section describes Uranus in each sign, including how we rebel, contribute to changing the world, and revolutionize the status quo. It also describes some of Uranus' effects historically as it moved through each sign. Uranus takes eighty-four years to orbit the Sun, and roughly seven years to move through a single sign. Because of this, Uranus affects us somewhat generationally. Anyone born within a seven-year period will have the same Uranus sign.

URANUS IN ARIES

(1928–1935, 2010–2019)

Generations with Uranus in Aries take the lead in changing society. Headstrong and individualistic, they are renegades who pave the way to new territory, crusading for freedom and independence. They are also pioneers in science and technology, with this placement showing up in the birth charts of legendary inventors Alexander Graham Bell and Thomas Edison. Aries rules war, and these generations innovate the military. Historically, they have been quite affected by the wars of their time, with the last generation growing up during World War II. Uranus in Aries also sparks abrupt changes in society, with the previous transit marking the end of the Roaring Twenties, the stock market crash, and the Great Depression. The most recent transit brought about ISIS as well as major political shocks and upheavals. Brexit passed unexpectedly in England, and Donald Trump won the United States presidential election, eliciting controversy and large-scale revolt.

URANUS IN TAURUS

(1935–1942, 2019–2025)

Generations with Uranus in Taurus could have shaky relationships to security and wealth, often experiencing childhood in the wake of economic upheaval. In fact, the last generation grew up during the Great Depression. These generations could either attempt to be free of material resources and financial obligations, or find creative ways of establishing security for themselves. Economically inventive, they have the potential to devise revolutionary systems around money and resources. Taurus rules cooking and farming, and these natives have historically generated original ideas about food and agriculture. The next transit could bring about financial and agricultural revolutions, and children with this placement could become leaders in changing our farming systems and solving issues of environmentalism.

URANUS IN GEMINI

(1942–1949, 2025–2033)

Generations with Uranus in Gemini revolutionize the way we think and communicate as a society. They establish technological innovations that help connect people, as well as advances in intellectual pursuits, like psychology, sociology, and metaphysics. They are inventors and inspired teachers, devising new and effective forms of education. Valuing free thought, they rebel against restrictive ideologies. In fact, the last Gemini-Uranus generation was integral to the hippie movement and the cultural revolution of the sixties. During Uranus's previous transits through Gemini, the Declaration of Independence was written and signed, Abraham Lincoln was elected president, and the Civil War began, which ended slavery in the United States.

URANUS IN CANCER

(1949–1956, 2033–2039)

Generations with Uranus in Cancer have novel ideas about home life and family, bucking against established traditions. They could have unstable families, or rebel against their parents, choosing much different paths than how they were raised. Sometimes these natives break away from their families altogether, or move to new countries, desiring absolute freedom from parental traditions and ties. Many people from the previous Cancer-Uranus generation became rebellious hippies. Cancer rules home while Uranus rules electronics, and this was a generation who grew up in homes where television was ubiquitous.

URANUS IN LEO

(1956–1961, 2039–2046)

Those with Uranus in Leo are original, creative, and expressive. They can make big impressions on the world, specifically revolutionizing the arts and entertainment. Their creativity is limitless. They have ample energy and ingenuity, which they easily apply to bringing their ideas into reality. Valuing freedom around love and sex, they find it difficult to commit to their families, and could feel compelled to leave their children, divorce, or have children outside the traditional family model. The last generation grew up during the cultural revolution of the sixties when family life altered in many ways. Madonna, Bill Gates, and Carl Jung were all born with Uranus in Leo. They revolutionized their respective fields, becoming extremely famous (Leo) for being inventive and original, and for contributing greatly to shifting the collective tides (Uranus).

URANUS IN VIRGO

(1961–1968, 2046–2053)

Generations born in the years of Uranus in Virgo discover revolutionary ways of relating to healing, health, and medicine. They often find cures to diseases and introduce new diets, methods of exercise, and alternative remedies. Uranus rules electricity, while Virgo rules practicality. When Uranus moved into Virgo, Thomas Edison invented practical electric light, and the Virgo-Uranus generation became the first to grow up in a world with electric light. Uranus in Virgo spawns excellent researchers who excel in the sciences, as they combine the insight of Uranus with Virgo's finely tuned intelligence. Albert Einstein, the legendary physicist, was born in a year when Uranus moved into Virgo. Sometimes, these natives must work to avoid repressing their authenticity, honoring the parts of themselves that long to be free.

URANUS IN LIBRA

(1968–1975, 2053–2059)

Generations with Uranus in Libra buck against traditions around marriage and relationships. Sometimes it's hard for these natives to settle down with one partner, tending toward divorce and multiple marriages. They also have unusual aesthetic tastes, helping to break creative molds and revolutionize the arts and culture. Since Libra rules law and equality, Libra-Uranus natives often become crusaders who fight to change policy and establish a more tolerant society. Libra-Uranus natives tend to grow up in times when peace is at stake and culture is rapidly changing. The last transit was a period of remarkable inventiveness in the Libran realms of art and music. The legendary music festival, Woodstock, occurred during this time, and music from the period continues to hold significant influence. Martin Luther King Jr. and Robert F. Kennedy were both assassinated during this transit, inciting protests and fights for equality. Vietnam War protests also occurred, when people joined forces (Uranus) to fight for peace (Libra).

URANUS IN SCORPIO

(1975–1981, 2059–2066)

Generations with Uranus in Scorpio alter the way society relates to spirituality, psychology, and the occult. Many leaders who transform the world have this placement. They become agents of change, healers, and extremists. Deep feelers, they possess great capacity to touch human suffering, and can pave the way toward collective rebirth. The current Scorpio-Uranus generation is working toward transforming our culture—leading us through the end of the current paradigm while clearing the way for the next.

URANUS IN SAGITTARIUS

(1981–1988, 2066–2072)

Generations with Uranus in Sagittarius introduce new philosophies and revolutionize religion. They break through blind faith and fundamentalism, establishing more genuine approaches to spirituality. They are travelers and explorers, eager to experience new places, people, and cultures. The current generation holds the potential to join humanity together in unifying belief systems and fundamental truths. They've shown a spike of interest in spirituality, while rebelling against organized religion.

URANUS IN CAPRICORN

(1988–1996, 2072-2079)

Generations with Uranus in Capricorn overturn outmoded traditions and oppressive governments, businesses, and leaders, replacing them with innovative, technologically sophisticated models. Rebelling against authority, they create new customs and systems that revolutionize society. Making up their own rules around commitment, they can transform the way we relate to marriage as a society. We are still witnessing how the current generation will step into this influence, but they are likely to redefine the very fabric of our society, becoming leaders in reforming our systems of government, economics, and morality, from the foundation of authenticity and integrity.

URANUS IN AQUARIUS

(1912–1920, 1996–2003)

Uranus rules Aquarius, and generations with Uranus in Aquarius are revolutionary souls, who make great strides in advancing humanity. Reformers and rebels, they come up with ingenious inventions and ideas around technology, science, and space travel. They sometimes struggle with intimacy in their one-on-one relationships, preferring to demonstrate love to their communities, groups of friends, and the world at large. During these transits, natives have grown up in the midst of revolutions in Mexico, China, and Russia, as well as the downfall of powerful monarchies during World War I. Legendary revolutionaries like Rosa Parks, John F. Kennedy, Nelson Mandela, and Joan of Arc all had Uranus in Aquarius.

URANUS IN PISCES

(1920–1928, 2003–2010)

Generations with Uranus in Pisces are mystical souls and revolutionaries in the realms of spirituality, film, music, and religion. Somewhat impractical, they can become lost in dreams and idealism. However, they plant important spiritual seeds, which are both innovative and unifying. The current generation could impart their enlightened vision of humanity to the rest of us, uniting us through a deeper understanding of unconditional love and oneness. Spiritual leaders like Jesus Christ and Pope John Paul II both had Uranus in Pisces, as well as the prophet Nostradamus, composer Wolfgang Amadeus Mozart, film legend Marlon Brando, and renowned photographer Diane Arbus.

NEPTUNE
SPIRITUALITY, COMPASSION, AND IMAGINATION

Neptune is the planet of spirituality and healing, helping us connect with life's invisible layers. Mystical, sensitive, and compassionate, it dissolves all boundaries, revealing our infinite nature. Ruling dreams and illusions, Neptune helps us to channel creativity. It is associated with the image-based and subtle arts, including music, poetry, dance, painting, photography, and film. While supremely gentle, Neptune is far from weak—its strength lies in the power of our imaginations and vulnerability. Neptune is a higher octave of Venus, planet of love. While Venus rules romance, Neptune is universal love for all beings.

People with Neptune forming harmonious aspects to their personal planets (see chapter 8) have the potential for tremendous empathy. They can heal others and connect with the higher realms. They are also likely to possess immense artistic, psychic, and spiritual gifts. With personal planets forming disharmonious aspects to Neptune, the same energy can become addiction and confusion. The Neptunian parts of our soul long to touch spirit, or an essence beyond suffering, which could either lead us to our spiritual path or unhealthy escapism.

Like Uranus and Pluto, Neptune requires Saturn's lessons to unlock its gifts. Before dissolving into limitless space, we must first develop our Saturnian discipline—rooting to the earth and committing fully to being human. Boundaries are necessary to protect this sensitive energy from slipping into misunderstanding or bewilderment. Idealistic and naive, Neptune sees the beauty in all beings. Without pragmatism, this perspective could lead to gullibility, impracticality, and delusion.

Since Neptune moves slowly, taking thirteen to fourteen years to move through a single sign, it affects us generationally and collectively. Neptune transits are particularly revealing of shifts in culture and the arts. The following section describes Neptune in each sign, including our imagination, spirituality, and where we are able to dissolve barriers. It also includes the artistic movements it inspired, which helped define the generations of each sign.

NEPTUNE IN ARIES

(1862–1875, 2025–2039)

With fiery imaginations, people with Neptune in Aries feel the urgent need to create and to help the less fortunate. These generations feel compelled to defend unity and compassion, and during the last Aries-Neptune period, people fought in the Civil War to end slavery and unify their country. The next transit begins in 2025, which could spark a period of elevated understanding. We may find ourselves banding together to fight for unification and compassionate ideals. Aries also rules combat, and Neptune rules photography. During the last transit, war photography became part of our cultural vernacular. Mathew Brady took his famous Civil War photographs, bringing home the reality of war to the public for the first time. The Salvation Army was also established—a charitable organization founded on spiritual ideals. Aries is direct, and realism dominated the arts during this era. Artists like Édouard Manet and authors like Leo Tolstoy revolted against the exaggerated emotional quality of romanticism, which preceded them, instead creating works that were true to life.

NEPTUNE IN TAURUS

(1875–1888, 2039–2052)

Generations with Neptune in Taurus have spiritual and idealistic values. Taurus rules the earth and our resources, which Neptune dissolves and transcends. Accordingly, these generations are able to rise above material limitations. In the nineteenth century, Taurus-Neptune natives grew up during the Long Depression—a worldwide economic recession. In art, impressionist painting reached its height. Neptune softens the boundaries of Taurean reality, and during this time, artists like Claude Monet and Pierre-Auguste Renoir experimented with blurry and open compositions. They depicted the undefined qualities of perception, moving away from direct realism. Symbolist artists and writers did the same, calling on synesthesia, where they sought to confound colors and the senses in their creative works. The upcoming transit begins in 2039, when we could find ourselves joining together (Neptune) to help heal the earth (Taurus). The future generation could become instrumental in making this happen.

NEPTUNE IN GEMINI

(1888–1902, 2052–2065)

Generations with Neptune in Gemini possess intellectual depth and broad imaginations. They work to dissolve barriers to education and literature. During the last Neptune in Gemini transit, the English focused on granting everyone access to the cultural arts, regardless of class. Oscar Wilde and George Bernard Shaw came into prominence during this period by writing plays that appealed to the masses. Very popular books like *Sherlock Holmes*, *The Jungle Book*, and *Dracula* were written during this transit as well. Gemini rules communication and Neptune rules film and unity, and this era saw the invention of the film projector, while great advances were made in communications technology. People from wide-spanning geographic locations were suddenly able to connect.

NEPTUNE IN CANCER

(1902–1915, 2065–2078)

Neptune in Cancer generations idealize the home, their inner lives, and cultural traditions. Sigmund Freud and Carl Jung were at the height of their careers during this period, applying their imaginations to the Cancerian topics of feelings and the deep unconscious. With Neptune in emotional Cancer, moody and sentimental art was the norm. Pablo Picasso entered his melancholic blue period, and Gustav Mahler composed emotionally charged and subtle symphonies. Cancer also rules family, and this period marked a golden age in children's books. Beatrix Potter published her famous *The Tale of Peter Rabbit* in the same year that this transit began.

NEPTUNE IN LEO

(1915–1928, 2078–2092)

Neptune in Leo generations produce charismatic leaders with strong visions and ideals. John F. and Robert Kennedy, Che Guevara, and Nelson Mandela were all born with this placement. Both Neptune and Leo are creative, popular, and expressive influences. The last time they joined forces marked an exciting era in culture when true artists became celebrities. Marcel Duchamp, Frida Kahlo, F. Scott Fitzgerald, Ernest Hemingway, and Georgia O'Keefe were leonine artists who became quite famous during this period, while Andy Warhol was born in the midst of it. This was also a momentous era for motion pictures, which began to dominate the entertainment industry. Acclaimed and influential performers like Charlie Chaplin, Buster Keaton, and Greta Garbo all became household names. Together, Neptune and Leo can enliven a party, and this period also included the flamboyant Roaring Twenties.

NEPTUNE IN VIRGO

(1928–1942, 2092–2105)

Neptune in Virgo generations channel their compassion into serving mankind. They are particularly interested in spiritual and physical healing. The last Virgo-Neptune generation was at the forefront of the civil rights movement, helping to rectify a harmful schism in humanity. During the transit, penicillin became ubiquitous; the National Cancer Institute was founded; and Christian Science, a denomination based on spiritual healing, became the fastest growing religion in the United States. As the planet of dreams moved through analytical Virgo, we also saw the height of surrealism in art. Painters like Salvador Dalí and

René Magritte analyzed dreams through their creative work. With Neptune in the sign of words and language, music became lyrics-driven. Billie Holiday, Fred Astaire, and Bing Crosby told stories through their widely popular songs. With Neptune dissolving Virgo's clarity and logic, this combination can cause widespread confusion. Two tumultuous events fulfilled this potential in the last transit—the Great Depression and World War II.

NEPTUNE IN LIBRA

(1942–1956)

Neptune in Libra generations hold high ideals around love and harmony. At the same time, Neptune can dissolve and undermine Libra's peace. During this transit, World War II and the Korean War were in effect, the atom bomb was invented, and the Cold War began. In art, painters and writers were expressing their desire for harmony. Mondrian created paintings that embodied abstract purity, and Antoine de Saint-Exupéry wrote *The Little Prince*, the famous and influential tale of a boy searching for inner peace and trying to understand love. The United Nations was also formed in this period, synchronizing world powers. Divorce rates sharply rose for this generation, who faced (and still face) disillusionment in their quest for perfect love.

NEPTUNE IN SCORPIO

(1956–1970)

Neptune in Scorpio generations are interested in mysticism, psychological transformation, and dissolving taboos. Scorpio investigates and destroys, and these generations fight for more transparent governments, working to dismantle abusive powers that harm the environment and humankind. During the last Neptune in Scorpio transit, the cultural revolution occurred, a fascinating period of growth, exploration, and transformation in the arts and culture. People began experimenting sexually and exploring the subconscious through mind-altering drugs. This was a breakthrough period in all of the arts, when musicians, choreographers, writers, and filmmakers reconceived their genres. In true Scorpio style, deconstructionism laid the foundation, as pop art, minimalism, and abstract art ripped open the definition of contemporary art. The movie *The Graduate* and Stan Brakhage's influential films explored cultural taboos, while Kurt Vonnegut's darkly satirical *Slaughterhouse-Five* became a bestseller, addressing the Scorpionic subjects of death, war, and trauma. Psychedelic art and music began to rule mainstream culture, with musicians like Jimi Hendrix, the Beatles, and the Grateful Dead becoming icons. Fascination with the occult, UFOs, and the supernatural became ubiquitous as well. Scorpio rules death, and during this transit, hospices were established, while Elisabeth Kübler-Ross published her famous book, *On Death and Dying.*

NEPTUNE IN SAGITTARIUS

(1970–1984)

People with Neptune in Sagittarius are broad-minded idealists. Their generations include powerful spiritual teachers, philosophers, intuitive healers, and truth seekers. They can dissolve fundamentalism and apply deep understanding and openness to cultures different from their own. The current generation has taken particular interest in Eastern religions and ancient wisdom practices like Buddhism, Taoism, yoga, and qigong. When the last transit began in 1970, spiritual teacher Chögyam Trungpa Rinpoche brought Tibetan Buddhism to the United States, capturing the attention of cultural heroes like Allen Ginsberg, Anne Waldman, and Joni Mitchell. Neptune rules delusion while Sagittarius rules dogma, and cults also became pervasive during this transit. Sagittarius represents strong beliefs, and in music, people were very much expressing their ideologies on stage. Punk rock and Rastafarianism grew in popularity, and Marvin Gaye's song "What's Going On," addressing police brutality, became one of the era's most celebrated songs.

NEPTUNE IN CAPRICORN

(1984–1998)

Neptune in Capricorn generations help to eliminate unnecessary walls and barriers. During this transit, the Soviet Union collapsed, and the Berlin wall came down, reunifying Germany. The current Capricorn-Neptune generation could become instrumental in dissolving the patriarchy. They blur tradition and find practical ways of applying spiritual insight toward helping the environment and creating more compassionate businesses, governments, and societies. Capricorn rules construction, and during the last transit, installation art was pervasive, consisting of large, three-dimensional works built on specific sites. In fact, when Neptune first moved into Capricorn, artist Donald Judd opened the Chinati Foundation in Marfa, Texas, which became a haven for many artists constructing large-scale pieces. In music, hard rock like Metallica and Slayer gained in popularity, correlating with Capricorn's steady intensity. Later in the transit, grunge took over popular culture, reflecting the dissolution of Capricorn's traditions and rules of decorum.

NEPTUNE IN AQUARIUS

(1998–2012)

Neptune in Aquarius generations propagate their humanitarian visions in order to help mankind. They are interested in establishing inclusive, compassionate, and spiritual communities, as well as technology that brings people together. In fact, the Internet became an integral part of mainstream culture during this transit. Aquarius rules electricity and community, and electronic music and interactive art soared in popularity. Festival culture became pervasive, as people came together in community to hear music and share in ideologies. In particular, Burning Man catapulted to fame—an annual gathering where people build makeshift communities consisting of interactive art and electronic music. Reflecting the nature of Neptune in Aquarius, these gatherings originally sought to embody values of egalitarianism, environmentalism, and spiritual growth. Since Neptune rules delusion and Aquarius rules community, the dangers for this era and generation are collective drug use and spiritual bypassing.

NEPTUNE IN PISCES

(2012–2026)

Neptune in Pisces generations are deeply spiritual. They strive to remove barriers between humans, bringing people together with compassionate inclusion. With psychic abilities and an innate understanding of oneness and interconnection, they could elevate our society to abide by more exalted ideals. During the current transit, yoga, ancient wisdom traditions, and mindfulness have become part of our everyday culture. Spiritual artists like Hilma af Klint and Emma

Kunz have reached posthumous fame, with people recognizing their work as ahead of its time. Spiritual music and musicians, like Kirtan and Krishna Das, have also become widely popular. Since Pisces rules delusion and Neptune is both the propagator and the dissolver, we have been experiencing widespread confusion, deception, and disillusionment in the media and politics. Time will tell how this transit continues to shape our future, but it could potentially hold seeds of globalism, unity, and expansion into higher consciousness.

PLUTO
SURRENDER, TRANSFORMATION, AND POWER

Pluto is the most powerful planet in astrology, ruling death, rebirth, and transformation. Known as "the destroyer," it ends a movement or generation and begins a new one when it moves from sign to sign. It reflects the struggles, passions, and metamorphoses of each generation.

Existing in the farthest reaches of our galaxy, Pluto helps us to achieve the pinnacle of spiritual advancement. With volcanic eruptions, it destroys anything out of alignment with truth. The birth of a baby, the death of a loved one, or a bad accident are all reflective of Pluto's intense lessons, leaving us bare to face our truest selves. Broader events like war, crisis, and the overturning of governments push us to experience the same Plutonian lessons as a collective.

Archetypically, Pluto is the shaman and Vajra master who requires wholehearted commitment to lead us to realization. We must dedicate ourselves to our spiritual growth, finding courage to look inward and leap into space—beyond concept, judgment, or fear. Pluto will help us to break out of our cocoons and step into the unknown. Whether we're hiding behind obsessions, addictions, power struggles, or toxic relationships, Pluto makes sure we abandon these illusions of safety, surrendering to the fires of self-awareness. At that point we will master the wisdom of Pluto—letting go, relaxing with uncertainty, and opening to change and transformation.

The slowest moving planet, Pluto orbits the Sun in 248-year cycles, taking an average of twenty years to move through a single sign.[1] When Pluto enters into a new sign, it marks the beginning of an era, defined by significant social changes. The following section describes the generations and eras associated with Pluto in each sign, including the challenges, obsessions, and breakthroughs of each.

PLUTO IN ARIES: THE EXPLORERS

(1822–1853, 2068–2098)

Generations with Pluto in Aries are courageous trailblazers and explorers. The last generation included the fiercely independent and foolhardy American pioneers who moved west to settle new territories. With Pluto in Aries spurring violent beginnings, this period was marked with bloodshed. This includes the Battle of the Alamo, Trail of Tears, and Mexican-American War. The gruesome events that befell the Donner-Reed Party also occurred during this period, when two families leading five hundred wagons to California hit an unexpected snowstorm, resorting to cannibalism to survive. In the future, this transit could mark a time when we begin to explore living on other planets, becoming pioneers in outer space.

---

[1] When there is crossover with the years, that is because Pluto retrograded into the previous sign and then returned to its current sign.

PLUTO IN TAURUS: THE TYCOONS

(1853–1884)

Generations with Pluto in Taurus are staunch and persevering, with keen focus on wealth, land, and possessions. Pluto in Taurus indicates battles for ownership, and this period saw the Civil War in the United States, when people fought and died to upend the right to possess other humans. Capitalism overtook feudalism throughout the world, and the Industrial Revolution sparked the creation of empires of wealth, in the form of monopolies and cartels. Plutocrats like Vanderbilt, Rockefeller, and Carnegie emerged on the scene, and the Gilded Age marked a period of rapid economic growth and opulence. Taurus rules singing, and during this period the Metropolitan Opera House was completed, which continues to be the largest classical music organization in North America.

PLUTO IN GEMINI: THE COMMUNICATORS

(1882–1914)

Pluto in Gemini generations are powerful communicators—writers, speakers, actors, and teachers. The people born during this period include legendary and gifted writers, like T. S. Eliot, William Faulkner, F. Scott Fitzgerald, and Ernest Hemingway, along with actors like Humphrey Bogart, Marlene Dietrich, Clark Gable, and Cary Grant. With Pluto's manipulative powers blending with Gemini's gifts of speech, two famous dictators were also born during this transit—Adolf Hitler and Mao Tse-tung. This period marked unparalleled advancement in communications technology, including inventions like the telephone, phonograph, motion pictures, and radio.

PLUTO IN CANCER: THE NUCLEAR FAMILIES

(1914–1939)

Pluto in Cancer generations are deeply emotional beings, with strong ties to family, home, and their countries. As destructive Pluto moved through security-driven Cancer, families across the world went through massive upheavals due to events like the Great Depression, World War I, and the Bolshevik Revolution. Cancer rules families and femininity, and we saw a massive restructuring of family life, with females beginning to work as men left for war. At this time, women also earned the right to vote in the United States. With Pluto in Cancer churning up the urge to self-protect, nationalism became ubiquitous, spurring the two world wars. When people born in this tumultuous era grew up, they helped to establish the Eisenhower era in the fifties, which changed the culture of family. The safety of cookie-cutter suburbia held mass appeal for these natives after enduring the shake-up of the Depression and world wars. Cancer rules the Moon, and two famous astronauts with Pluto in Cancer became the first to land on the Moon—Neil Armstrong and Buzz Aldrin.

PLUTO IN LEO: THE PLEASURE SEEKERS

(1937–1958)

Pluto in Leo generations are intensely creative, playful, and pleasure seeking. People born during this transit sparked the sexual revolution and mainstream recreational drug use. Leo rules children, and this generation included the baby boomers, named for the sharp increase of births after World War II. Marked by authoritarianism, the Leo-Pluto period endured major abuses of power. McCarthyism ruined many people's lives, and Arthur Miller's famous play *The Crucible* compared it to the Salem witch trials. Quite remarkably, those trials began in 1692, the last year Pluto moved into Leo. Pluto rules death, while Leo rules celebrity, and many famous people with Pluto in Leo died young—including Janis Joplin, Jimi Hendrix, Brian Jones, Jim Morrison, and John Lennon. This generation's tremendous creative output spawned numerous cultural and artistic movements. Obsessed with fame, they viewed celebrities as heroes to be worshipped and passionately adored.

PLUTO IN VIRGO: THE PRAGMATISTS

(1956–1972)

Generations with Pluto in Virgo are down-to-earth pragmatists. They value the environment and work hard to acquire wealth. In some ways, they rebelled against the pleasure seeking of the wilder generation before them. Virgo rules health, and these natives care deeply about fitness and well-being. They revolutionized medical technology, invented workout videos, and made alternative medicine mainstream. These were the clean-cut preppies as well as the crunchy hippies—both Virgoan archetypes. Environmentalists, they set a new cultural standard for organic food and recycling. Virgo is opposite of spiritual Pisces, and this generation has been largely anti-religion, popularizing atheism and leading the rebellion against religious hypocrisy. Virgo rules purity and service, and throughout the sixties, people fought for worthy ideals, working tirelessly to serve mankind. Since Pluto rules death, we also saw the assassinations of noble souls working in service of humanity, including John F. Kennedy and Martin Luther King Jr. In the future, this generation will hopefully lead us to solve our environmental and healthcare problems.

PLUTO IN LIBRA: THE EGALITARIANS

(1971–1984)

Pluto in Libra generations are concerned with fairness, equality, and justice. These are the Gen Xers, known for their Libran laziness, fickleness, and trouble settling down. Venus rules Libra, planet of femininity, and this transit marked an era when women were sexually free without shame. This generation invented metrosexuality, blurring the lines of female and male, in true Libra fashion. Libra rules art, and throughout this transit, art helped to generate major social transformation. Libra also rules peace, and the Vietnam War came to an end, while China and the United States made peace after existing as hostile powers for a long time. People with this transit have led the way in establishing LGBTQ rights, and in redefining marriage and dating. Marked by trouble with relationships, divorce rates reached an all-time high during this transit. In the future, this generation could lead the way in changing our legal and justice systems.

PLUTO IN SCORPIO: THE REVOLUTIONARIES

(1735–1747, 1983–1995)

Pluto in Scorpio generations are imaginative, psychic, and willful. Powerful revolutionaries, they show up at the end of each era, breaking us free of oppressive powers while leading us to collective rebirth. During the eighteenth century, people born during this transit fought in the Revolutionary War. During the most recent transit, the USSR and Berlin Wall collapsed, ending communism. When Pluto was in Scorpio in the fifteenth century, Christopher Columbus discovered the Americas, establishing the New World. Before that, this transit occurred at the beginning and end of the Crusades, which concluded the Dark Ages, and cleared the way for the Renaissance. The current generation is known as the Millennials. Scorpio rules sex, and they have smashed through sexual taboos and embraced bisexuality, open relationships, and sexual freedom. They are attuned to the invisible, and catapulted the magical *Harry Potter* book series to fame. As we enter the new age, set to begin in January of 2020, when Jupiter, Saturn, and Pluto join together, this generation will lead us through the end of the industrial age and into a new one—stepping up as leaders with inherent bravery, depth, and power.

PLUTO IN SAGITTARIUS: THE TRUTH REVEALERS

(1747–1762, 1995–2008)

Pluto in Sagittarius generations are freedom-loving and adventurous spirits who have disdain for authority. Outgoing and irrepressible, they crusade for their beliefs, exposing and propagating truth. During the last Sagittarius-Pluto transit, the Central Intelligence Agency admitted that the United States had lied to the world about why they invaded Iraq. Pluto rules sex, while Sagittarius rules truth, and two sex scandals rocked the world during the last transit—the Clinton-Lewinsky scandal and the cover-ups of pedophilia in the Catholic Church. Sagittarius is a social sign, and social media was invented during this period, quickly taking hold of mainstream culture. As this generation reaches maturity, they may become leaders in dismantling harmful religious institutions, or at least bringing them into a revolutionary new phase. With openness and curiosity, they have more interest in genuine spiritual experience than religious dogma.

PLUTO IN CAPRICORN: THE BUILDERS

(1762–1778, 2008–2024)

Pluto in Capricorn generations will work to overthrow tyranny and establish new governments, ruling structures, and traditions. During this transit in the eighteenth century, the founding fathers signed the Declaration of Independence, which marked the birth of the United States and the beginning of a freer form of democratic government, to be ruled by the people. Pluto's recent transit through Capricorn has been marked by political upheaval and an overturning of patriarchal traditions. Time will tell how this plays out, but in the future, the Capricorn-Pluto generation could help us establish new traditions, paradigms, and systems of government. We might even see a rebirth of the United States as Pluto returns to the same degree as its conception.

PLUTO IN AQUARIUS: THE FUTURISTS

(1778–1798, 2024–2044)

The Pluto in Aquarius generations are humanitarians with high values. They tout democracy and work to help the underdogs. When Pluto last transited Aquarius, the French Revolution occurred, which triggered the dismantling of global monarchies and subsequent establishment of republics and liberal democracy. Aquarius rules technology and the future, and Aquarius-Pluto periods are ones of great scientific advancement. The last transit marked the beginning of the Industrial Revolution—a major turning point in humanity that improved the quality of life for the general population. The Age of Enlightenment also coincided with this period, promoting Aquarian reason and scientific thinking. Philosopher Immanuel Kant had far-reaching influence on European philosophy, promoting the belief that we can achieve peace through universal democracy and international cooperation. The future transit will likely correlate with a great surge in technology, when humans may begin merging with computers, as Ray Kurzweil and many other contemporary thinkers have predicted. When Pluto moves into Aquarius in 2024, it will signify the beginning of the Age of Aquarius—meant to bring collective enlightenment, progressive values, cooperation, and freedom from oppression.

PLUTO IN PISCES: THE SPIRITUAL ARTISTS

(1797–1823, 2044–2068)

Generations with Pluto in Pisces focus intently on spirituality, art, and culture. The last transit marked a period of great romanticism in the arts, when renowned poets Lord Byron, John Keats, and Percy Shelley created seminal works, while Beethoven composed his legendary symphonies. Painters like John Constable wanted to paint with deep, Piscean sensitivity to nature, and he began disregarding the importance of line, painting instead with free patches of color. Pisces rules the ocean, and the first submarine was built during this transit, while many immigrants traveled across seas to the New World. When Pluto reenters Pisces, we may see a highly artistic and spiritual period, along with an influx of spiritual leaders who promote compassion and tolerance. We could experience increased globalism and the continued disintegration of cultural and racial barriers. Overall, this generation is set to be spiritual, loving, and broad-minded.

8

THE HOUSES

Where We Direct Our Energies

AFTER LEARNING about the planets and signs, we now reach the third building block of astrology: the houses. While the planets and signs represent innate facets of ourselves—how we think, love, and feel—the houses are the areas in life where we apply these energies.

The twelve houses represent twelve categories of life that originated over two thousand years ago, in the Babylonian times. The Babylonians believed that life consisted of a range of activities and domains where we apply ourselves, each correlating with a particular house. Money, creativity, marriage, career, and spirituality were all included in these categories.

On a literal level, the houses represent positions in the sky. The first house begins at the easternmost horizon at the time of our birth. Let's consider a certain planet—the Moon. Where was the Moon in the sky at the moment we were born? Was it over our heads? To the east? If the Moon were on the easternmost horizon or just below it, that means it would fall in our first house. If it were directly below us, or slightly west of that, the Moon would fall in our fourth house. If it were just above our heads, or slightly to the east, it would fall in our tenth house.

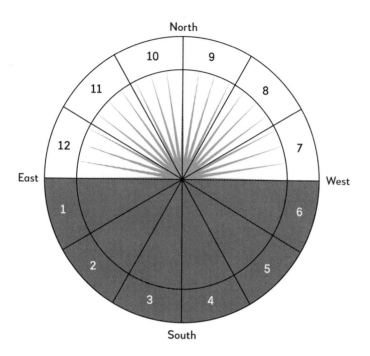

The twelve houses not only correspond with twelve categories of life, but also with the twelve signs. The sign that matches each house is called its *natural ruler*. Knowing the natural ruler of a house helps to elucidate its meaning. While the house and sign do not hold the exact same meaning, they do share similar qualities. For example, the second house represents money and its natural ruler is resourceful Taurus; the seventh house represents marriage and partnership and its natural ruler is romantic Libra; and the tenth house represents career and its natural ruler is industrious Capricorn.

HOUSE	NATURAL RULER
First House: Self	Aries
Second House: Possessions	Taurus
Third House: Communication	Gemini
Fourth House: Home	Cancer
Fifth House: Creativity	Leo
Sixth House: Service	Virgo
Seventh House: Partnership	Libra
Eighth House: Sex and Death	Scorpio
Ninth House: Philosophy	Sagittarius
Tenth House: Career	Capricorn
Eleventh House: Community	Aquarius
Twelfth House: Spirituality	Pisces

Let's look at a couple of planets in the houses to clarify how they work. If the Sun, our basic identity and self, falls in the seventh house of partnerships, we might identify strongly with our relationships; we could be prone to feeling that our confidence (the Sun) depends heavily on validation from our partnerships. If our Moon, planet of emotions, were in the second house of possessions, then luxuries and material security would feel extra important to our sense of contentment and emotional well-being.

The following chapter outlines the meaning of each house, along with other important features of the zodiac. Don't worry if this feels confusing or abstract at first. The houses become clearer when we begin weaving everything together in chapter 10.

THE HOUSES

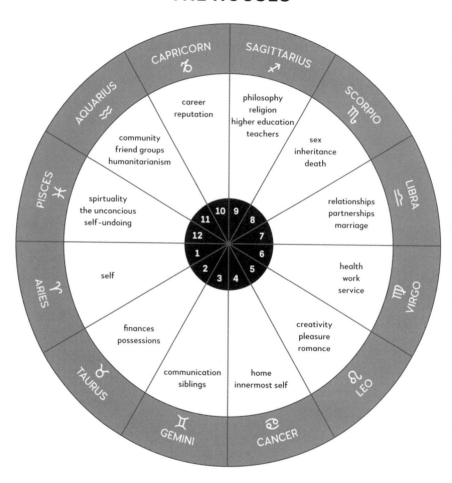

FIRST HOUSE: SELF

NATURAL RULER **Aries**

KEYWORDS *self-image, physical body, style, mannerisms, likes and dislikes*

The first house rules the self, confidence, and basic expression. Whichever signs and planets fall in the first house indicate how others see us and how we relate to the outer world. The planets that show up in the first house are obvious to everyone we meet. We wear those energies on our sleeve. This house affects the rest of our chart, operating as an entry point into the entirety of our lives and beings. It also represents our body and outward appearance. For example, if the sign Capricorn fell in a person's first house, she would come across as reserved, traditional, and ambitious; if the Sun fell in the first house, it would indicate star quality.

SECOND HOUSE: WEALTH

NATURAL RULER **Taurus**

KEYWORDS *possessions, money and wealth, resources, property and real estate, mastery, self-worth*

The second house rules wealth and material possessions. It indicates what will be lucrative for us and how we make money. Many planets in the second house would indicate ample material security, beautiful possessions, and creature comforts. These natives are able to be resourceful and can focus on becoming masters of their trade. They manifest abundance and work toward developing a healthy sense of self-worth. The planets and signs that fall in the second house reveal our relationships to wealth and livelihood. For example, with the sign Libra falling in the second house, one could make money off art or aesthetic abilities; the planet Jupiter in the second house would indicate luck with manifestation.

THIRD HOUSE: COMMUNICATION

NATURAL RULER **Gemini**

KEYWORDS *communication, speaking, writing, early education, siblings, aunts and uncles, neighbors, short trips*

The third house rules communication of all kinds. With many planets in the third house, one could be a writer, teacher, or public speaker. The third house also rules early education and short trips, in addition to siblings, aunts, uncles, and neighbors. Whatever planets and signs fall in this house reveal how we communicate. For example, a third house in Cancer would denote a knack for public speaking—the ability to feel into the energy of the room and speak from the heart; Venus in the third house would represent poetic abilities, with a halo of beauty surrounding the native's words.

FOURTH HOUSE: HOME

NATURAL RULER **Cancer**

KEYWORDS *relationship with parents, how you nurture, motherhood, the mother, childhood, innermost self, intimacy, home life*

The fourth house is our innermost realm—our private world that we only sometimes share with others. This is the source of our deepest feelings, intimacy, and nurturing. While the second house rules the tangible home, the fourth house is the feeling of home as well as familiarity and our mother. It also indicates motherhood in general, or how we nurture children. The planets and signs that fall in the fourth house reveal how we relate to intimacy and nurturing. A Leo fourth house would signify someone who is warm and affectionate when they're close to another person; Uranus in the fourth house could mean an unusual relationship to the mother or motherhood in general.

FIFTH HOUSE: CREATIVITY AND ROMANCE

NATURAL RULER **Leo**

KEYWORDS *creativity, pleasure, children, true love, love affairs, entertainment, where you give your heart and affections*

The fifth house is the house of creativity, playfulness, and true love. It is also how we entertain ourselves and what brings us pleasure. With many planets in the fifth house, we would have an abundance of creative energy, playfulness, and affection. We might have many love affairs or lovers throughout our lives, easily diving into joyful romantic expression. The planets and signs in the fifth house reveal how we relate to creativity and love. For example, a Capricorn fifth house could mean making a living off our creative work, or relating traditionally to love; Mercury in the fifth house could signify an ability to perform, or a tendency to apply our mental abilities toward creative self-expression.

SIXTH HOUSE: SERVICE AND HEALTH

NATURAL RULER **Virgo**

KEYWORDS *health, service, work, worries*

The sixth house rules health, work, and service toward others. It can also reveal what we worry about. With many planets in the sixth house, natives would be high-strung and helpful. Devoted and service-oriented, they apply their energies toward working hard for the benefit of others. The signs and planets that fall in the sixth house tell us about our work ethic and what we devote ourselves to. The sixth house in Aries would indicate a conscientious leader who is humble and unafraid of hard work; the Moon in the sixth house reveals a devoted spirit who finds contentment in daily routines and assisting others.

SEVENTH HOUSE: PARTNERSHIP AND MARRIAGE

NATURAL RULER **Libra**

KEYWORDS *romantic partnerships, husband or wife, marriage, ability to work harmoniously with others, open enemies or adversaries, ideal partner, shadow self*

The seventh house rules relationships and marriage. It reveals our shadow selves and ideal partners. Many planets in the seventh house indicate an emphasis on relationships, overidentifying with others, and codependence. Ironically, this house also indicates open enemies. The signs and planets that fall in the seventh house show how we relate to relationships and marriage. For example, Capricorn in the seventh house means that natives tend to marry traditionally; Uranus in the seventh house could mean an unusual approach to love, or difficulties stabilizing committed relationships.

EIGHTH HOUSE: SEX, DEATH, AND BIRTH

NATURAL RULER **Scorpio**

KEYWORDS *sex, death, inheritance, deep psychological work, birth, rebirth, healing, mysticism*

The eighth house is the house of death, sex, birth, and psychology. Many planets here indicate the push toward deep inner work and transformation. Perhaps these natives would be therapists, shamans, hospice workers, or doulas. Sexuality is emphasized, as well as investigation, and digging into the hidden aspects of human experience. The planets and signs that fall in the eighth house indicate, foremost, how we relate to sexual intimacy. For example, Sagittarius in the eighth house would reflect a person who may want to explore sexual intimacy with many people, or at least people from different backgrounds; Mars in the eighth house could lead to a deep sexual nature and powerful desires. Since the eighth house also rules inheritance, the lucky planet Jupiter falling in the eighth house could signify family money.

NINTH HOUSE: PHILOSOPHY AND ADVENTURE

NATURAL RULER **Sagittarius**

KEYWORDS *philosophy, higher education, adventure, travel to faraway places, religion, exploration of different cultures, teachers, gurus*

The ninth house rules travel to foreign countries, spiritual teachers, and higher education. With many planets in this house, one could feel compelled to travel, live in faraway countries, or seek adventure. A ninth house emphasis could also lead to an academic path—graduate school or a life of philosophical inquiry. The planets and signs that fall in the ninth house indicate how we relate to religion and philosophy. For example, Aries in the ninth house could reveal a courageous and well-traveled spirit, as well as the willingness to dive headlong into any adventure; Jupiter in the ninth house could signify great achievements when pursuing higher education, the ability to teach, or luck finding a spiritual teacher or inspiring mentors and professors.

TENTH HOUSE: CAREER AND SOCIAL STATUS

NATURAL RULER **Capricorn**

KEYWORDS *career, social status, the father, fatherhood, ambition, outer responsibilities*

The tenth house rules career, society, and the father. This is the house that shows us which career will bring success and how we will contribute to society. It can also tell us about how we perceive our father and how we relate to discipline and tradition. Many planets here would mean we focus our energies on climbing the social ladder, achieving success, and becoming well known. The signs and planets that fall in this house indicate how we relate to career and society. For example, a tenth house in Gemini reflects a soul who could make a living as a writer, teacher, or speaker; Pluto in the tenth house denotes a commanding presence at work, and the potential to achieve tremendous power and fame.

ELEVENTH HOUSE: FRIENDS AND COMMUNITY

NATURAL RULER **Aquarius**

KEYWORDS *groups of friends, community, humanitarianism, clubs, enlightened society, goals, hopes, and wishes*

The eleventh house rules community, friendship, and humanitarianism. In particular, it tells us about our peer groups and the types of friends that we attract. If Cancer falls in our eleventh house, we could have many friends who are healers and nurturers; if Mars falls in our eleventh house, we could be a leader in our community, or a pioneer who fights for humanitarian purposes. Many planets in the eleventh house denote an individual who focuses their talents on community, creating enlightened society, bringing people together, and crusading for human rights.

TWELFTH HOUSE: SPIRITUALITY AND THE SUBCONSCIOUS

NATURAL RULER **Pisces**

KEYWORDS *spirituality, the subconscious, addictions, escapism, karma, psychic abilities, meditation, unconscious energies, photography, film, fantasy, illusions*

The twelfth house is traditionally known as the house of self-undoing. It rules addiction, escapism, and our unconscious drives. On the flip side, it also represents spirituality, psychic abilities, and unconditional love. With many planets in the twelfth house, someone could feel driven by many subconscious impulses. Choosing to exert this energy toward spiritual pursuits, retreats, or meditation, this same person could go quite far on their spiritual path. Also ruling film, photography, and spiritual arts, a prominent twelfth house could reveal talents in these domains. The signs and planets that fall in the twelfth house show what we keep hidden. For example, Pisces in the twelfth house could mean unrealized or underdeveloped spirituality; Uranus in the twelfth house signifies someone who keeps their eccentricity hidden.

THE FOUR HOUSE CUSPS
ASCENDANT, DESCENDANT, NADIR, AND MIDHEAVEN

The most significant angles of the chart are the angular house cusps, correlating with the first, fourth, seventh, and tenth houses. If planets touch these angles, they have particular significance in our lives and beings, and their meaning in our chart is amplified.

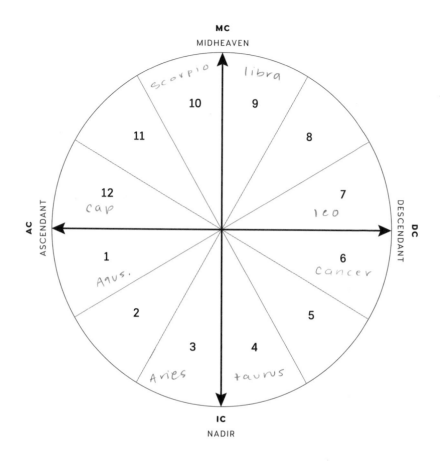

THE ASCENDANT (FIRST HOUSE CUSP)
outermost self / physical appearance

THE DESCENDANT (SEVENTH HOUSE CUSP)
relationships / marriage

THE NADIR, OR IMUM COELI (FOURTH HOUSE CUSP)
innermost self / intimacy

THE MIDHEAVEN, OR MEDIUM COELI (TENTH HOUSE CUSP)
career / reputation

HOUSE DIVISIONS

The houses are divided into four hemispheric quadrants—Eastern, Western, Northern, and Southern. The positions are counterintuitive, corresponding with the opposite hemisphere that we would imagine. The Eastern is the left half, the Western is the right; the Northern Hemisphere is the bottom half, the Southern is the top. When looking at a chart, the hemispheric emphasis can be determined by where the majority of planets fall in a person's chart. Each emphasis has a different meaning.

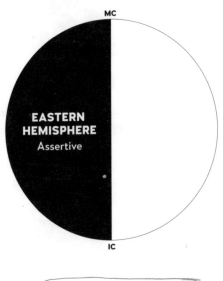

Eastern Hemisphere: Assertive

The Eastern Hemisphere consists of the houses on the left side of a chart. People with the majority of planets in the Eastern Hemisphere tend to be self-motivated, demonstrating initiative, independence, and assertiveness.

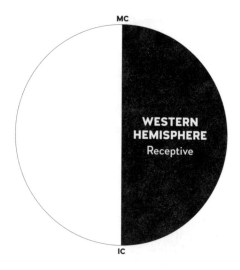

Western Hemisphere: Receptive

The Western Hemisphere consists of the houses on the right side of a chart. People with the majority of planets in the Western Hemisphere tend to be more receptive and oriented toward others.

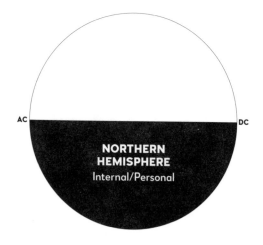

The Northern Hemisphere: Internal/Personal

The Northern Hemisphere consists of the bottom half of a chart. These are the internal and subjective houses. With many planets in the Northern Hemisphere, natives are likely to be introverted and private, orienting toward self-improvement and internal development.

The Southern Hemisphere: External/Social

The Southern Hemisphere consists of the top half of chart. These are the more social and external houses, which orient toward the collective. With many planets in the Southern Hemisphere, natives are likely to be more extroverted, with an emphasis on external events and the public domain.

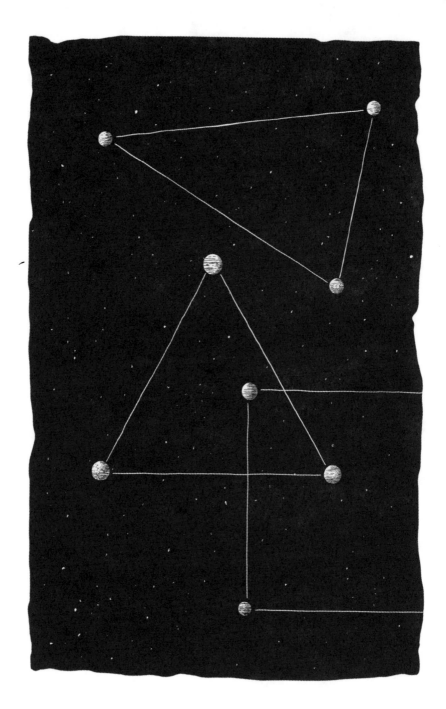

9

THE ASPECTS

Relationships between Planets

AFTER LEARNING about the planets, signs, and houses, the final component necessary for reading a birth chart is the aspects. These are the angles formed between two or more planets in our birth chart, indicating how our planetary energies relate to each other. They explain how different facets of our personality harmonize and blend—or how they create paradox, tension, and complexity.

The aspects fall into two broad categories—major and minor. The major aspects represent the strongest degrees between two planets or points in our chart. The most important major aspect is the conjunction, which is roughly 0° between two planets.

Both major and minor aspects are further categorized as harmonious or disharmonious. However, there is no such thing as a "bad" angle. The tense or disharmonious aspects (like squares and oppositions) are what give us passion, intensity, and drive. If we had only harmonious aspects (like trines and sextiles) in our chart, we might be complacent souls—content vegging out, rarely challenging the status quo. Our disharmonies are what propel us forward, lending us drive to resolve tension through action, creativity, and ambition.

In learning to read astrology charts, we do not have to memorize the meaning of every aspect between individual planets. If we know the significance of the aspects in general, we can apply that to what we know about the planets and signs. For example, let's say that someone's Venus forms a trine, or 120° angle, to the Ascendant. A trine is a harmonious angle; Venus represents love and beauty; and the Ascendant is our outer appearance. Weaving this information together, we can expect this native to come across as charming, beautiful, and magnetic. If we know that her Ascendant is in Aquarius, that would deepen our understanding even further. Perhaps this person appears eccentric or idiosyncratic (Ascendant in Aquarius), but with a harmonious angle to Venus, she would be popular in her rebellion. She wouldn't be an awkward outcast or confrontational rebel, which can sometimes accompany an Aquarius Ascendant. On the other hand, if Mars, planet of virility and anger, were conjunct her Aquarius Ascendant, she could seem significantly more aggressive, defiantly expressing her otherness and contrarianism.

Understanding the angles, we can begin to piece together our deeper complexities. Our portraits begin to refine as we discover how our potentials work together in a cohesive whole—how they create friction and how they flow, where we have natural talents and where we need to work harder. These are the more specific details of our psyches that make us who we are, shaping the arc of our personalities and lives. This chapter outlines the major and minor aspects and the meaning of each.

The following are considered to be the major aspects, or the most significant angles between two planets:

ANGLE	SYMBOL	DESCRIPTION	+/-
Conjunction 0°	♂	Strongest aspect, intensification of energies	Neither positive nor negative
Trine 120°	△	Easy blend of energies	Most harmonious aspect
Opposition 180°	♂	Tension, friction, passion	Disharmonious
Sextile 60°	✳	Beneficial, but weaker than trine	Harmonious
Square 90°	□	Difficult angle, friction and struggle	Disharmonious

♂ Conjunction
0°

Two planets falling in the same degree of the same sign, or within 10° of each other

This is the strongest aspect between two planets or points. This angle is neither positive nor negative. It simply intensifies the energy of each planet. It also means that those energies will work together inextricably in the native's personality. If someone has a conjunction in their chart between two or more planets, this point on their chart will be an emphasis in their personality and life trajectory. If the conjunction is exact to the degree, the influence is more powerful.

Trine
120°

Two planets falling 120° apart, or within 9° of that in either direction

This is the most harmonious aspect between two planets. Energies blend easily and harmoniously. With too many trines in a chart, one could be complacent or lazy—content with little action or effort.

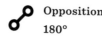 **Opposition**
180°

Two planets falling 180° apart, or within 9° of that in either direction

This aspect is considered disharmonious, with two opposing energies creating tension and friction. This discordance can generate dynamic, creative passion, which eventually leads to growth and intrigue. Harmonizing the polarities is part of the native's life path.

 Sextile
60°

Two planets falling 60° apart, or within 6° of that in either direction

This aspect is considered harmonious, though it is weaker than the trine. More effort is required to access the benefits.

 Square
90°

Two planets falling 90° apart, or within 9° of that in either direction

This aspect is considered quite difficult and disharmonious, indicating friction and obstacles. These challenges eventually build character and lead to wisdom, drive, and depth.

MINOR ASPECTS

The following are known as the minor aspects, since they hold less power and significance than the major aspects:

ANGLE	SYMBOL	DESCRIPTION	+/-
Quincunx 150°	⚻	Energies cannot merge	Challenging
Semisquare 45°	∠	Less potent version of square	Mildly disharmonious
Sesquisquare 135°	⚼	Similar to semisquare	Mildly disharmonious
Semisextile 30°	⚺	Less potent version of sextile	Mildly harmonious

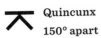 **Quincunx**
150° apart
Two planets falling 150° apart, or within 2° of that in either direction

This aspect can be challenging. With the square and opposition, it is difficult to merge the energy of two planets, but with the quincunx, the planets simply cannot be merged. Because of this, there is a tendency to compartmentalize. For example, Venus-quincunx-Saturn could mean that our romantic and professional lives are difficult to blend, and we may find it difficult to feel satisfied in both domains simultaneously. With Venus ruling values, we could also find our work at odds with our sense of ethics.

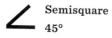 **Semisquare**
45°

Two planets falling 45° apart, or within 2° of that in either direction

Mildly disharmonious. A less potent version of the square.

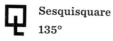 **Sesquisquare**
135°

Two planets falling 135° apart, or within 2° of that in either direction

Mildly disharmonious. Similar to the semisquare.

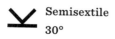 **Semisextile**
30°

Two planets falling 30° apart, or within 2° of that in either direction

Mildly harmonious. A less potent version of the sextile.

ASPECT PATTERNS

When looking at birth charts, we may notice patterns of angles between planets or points, forming specific shapes—such as a perfect triangle, a square, or even a kite. These are called **aspect patterns**. The planets or points involved in an aspect pattern form dynamic relationships with each other, the energies working together with mutual influence. Aspect patterns can be either harmonious or challenging. However, just like with aspects, the challenging patterns hold great potential. They lend depth and drive to natives, triggering great effort and life struggles that ultimately reveal their gifts. And while the harmonious aspect pattern indicates positive karma and natural talents, outside stimulus is required for natives to activate their potentials.

Here are several key aspect patterns in a birth chart, along with their meaning:

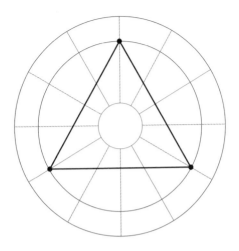

Grand Trine

A Grand Trine is an equilateral triangle, formed by three trines, or 120° angles. This pattern represents an easy flow of energies and natural gifts. Just by being, natives with Grand Trines will bring balance and harmony to whoever is around them. However, work is necessary to unlock their gifts. Idleness or complacency sometimes accompany this aspect pattern, since natives can feel contentment more easily than others. If another planet forms a challenging angle to any point of the Grand Trine, that will help to mobilize the native's gifts.

Typically, the three points, or planets, involved in a Grand Trine will fall in a single element: fire, earth, air, or water. Grand Trines in fire represent gifts of inspiration, passion, or athleticism; earth Grand Trines represent the gifts of grounding, stability, pragmatism, and sensuality; air signs bring talents of the mind, communication, logic, and wit; and water Grand Trines endow natives with natural empathy and the ability to nurture, emotionally support, and heal others.

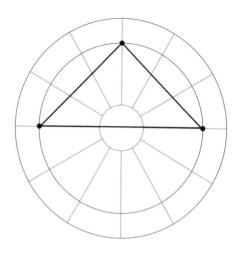

T-Square

A T-Square is a right triangle, formed by one opposition (180° angle), and two squares (90° angles). This aspect pattern represents powerful struggles and drive, which can lead to great suffering, as well as considerable achievement. Natives release the tension of their opposition through the tip of the triangle, known as the focal point. They will apply themselves rigorously to whatever activities and energies the focal point represents. This can lead to great passion, periods of intense work, and an almost desperate thrust into that area of life.

The energy of the T-Square comes in erratic bursts, and requires ample recharging. The key to finding balance is to develop the energies of the empty quadrant—whatever house or sign is opposite the focal point. This can provide great relief and equilibrium for the T-Square native.

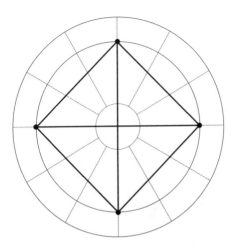

Grand Cross

A Grand Cross is a square, formed by two oppositions (180° angles) and four squares (90° angles). This aspect pattern represents remarkable gifts, accompanied by great struggles and inflexibility. Life's challenges hold the key to unlocking these natives' potentials. They are gifted in disparate areas of life and sometimes find it challenging to pick one direction. In a way, they are forced to find center, balance, and harmony, otherwise they will remain plagued by inner tensions. As they continue along their journeys, both inner and outer, facing their deep work and fears, they have the incredible capacity to become accomplished and significant people in the world.

Stellium

A Stellium occurs when three or more planets fall in a single sign or house. This aspect pattern indicates an extreme focus on the affairs or tendencies of this house or sign. The native is able to direct tremendous drive, self-development, awareness, and activity toward these areas of life. They could look to the opposite sign or house to learn how to find balance and equilibrium.

10

WEAVING IT ALL TOGETHER

H AVING LEARNED about the signs, planets, houses, and aspects, we have all the rudimentary pieces necessary to begin reading charts. Since astrology is primarily an intuitive art, each astrologer will have his or her own style or methodology. But here, I provide what I've found to be the most helpful and direct approach to beginning chart reading.

Granted, this can seem overwhelming at first. There are many moving pieces and concepts to grasp. But if we break it down into simple steps, it will begin to make more sense. Remember that astrology is a language, and it takes practice to become fluent. The more charts you read, the better you will become.

Here, we will apply the basic steps of chart reading to an example chart—that of legendary musician, songwriter, and poet, Leonard Cohen. Then we will apply the steps to your own chart.

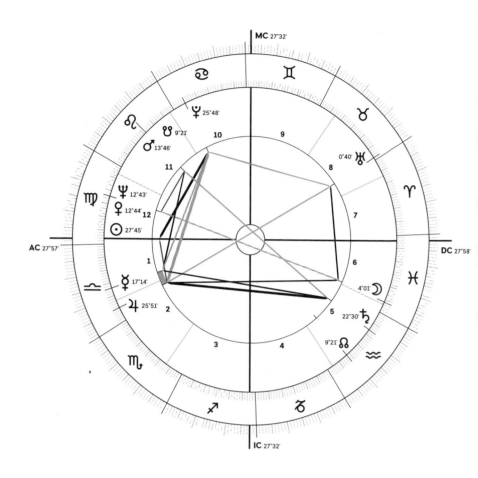

LEONARD COHEN

September 21, 1934 | 6:45 AM

Montreal, Quebec, Canada

BASIC STEPS OF CHART READING

STEP 1: CHART EMPHASIS

First, let's get a feel for his primary energies by evaluating the chart emphasis. Where are most of Leonard Cohen's planets in his chart? We can see that the majority of planets are in the left quadrant, or Eastern Hemisphere (see chapter 8). This gives us an idea of Cohen's basic drives—his self-motivation, initiative, independence, and assertiveness—before we unpack the rest of his chart.

STEP 2: THE SUN, MOON, AND ASCENDANT

Now let's look at the three most important elements of any chart: the Sun, Moon, and Ascendant. First, we see that his Sun, or basic personality, is in Virgo; his Moon, or emotional nature, is in Pisces; and his Ascendant, or social mask, is also in Virgo. *(Aries)*

(aquarius)

Sun, or Basic Ego *cap*

Virgo: the humble servant, logical organizer, careful wordsmith,
devotee, striving for simplicity and purity

With his Sun, or basic personality, in Virgo, we can see that Cohen clearly demonstrated the traits of his Sun sign. He was an incredibly gifted writer and poet, who lived modestly and strived toward purity. While he was known for writing beautiful and simple songs with exquisite lyrics, his basic demeanor was simple and deferential, and he devoted himself wholeheartedly to his Buddhist teacher.

THE SUN'S HOUSE PLACEMENT *IV*

First house: basic expression

Sun in the first house tells us that even though Cohen was a Virgo, who typically works behind the scenes to support other people, he applied his Virgoan energies to the first house of basic expression—the house of confidence and being seen. So although he was a shy Virgo, he had confidence, assertiveness, and star quality. He could own his awkwardness, nerdiness, and perfectionism, and embody it with flair.

Moon, or Inner Self (a r i e s)
Pisces: the mystic, dreamer, spiritualist, striving for oneness

Next, what do we know about Cohen's Moon? It's in Pisces, the opposite sign to his Sun and Ascendant. This means that while his outer identity (Sun and Ascendant in Virgo) was defined by hard work, language, and precision, at heart he was a mystic, with a vivid imagination and spiritual inclinations. This was true of Cohen, who practiced Zen Buddhism and Judaism, and who drew from his deep imagination and spiritual longings.

THE MOON'S HOUSE PLACEMENT 2
Sixth house: service, devotion, and hard work

With his Moon in Pisces, we know that at heart, Cohen was a spiritualist and a dreamer. But where did he apply these energies? The sixth house is associated with Virgo, ruling service, hard work, and devotion. Again, we know that he was a devout Jew and Buddhist and that he worked hard toward expressing his sometimes-otherworldly music. Virgo is also ascetic, and Cohen gave up luxuries to live monastically and study under his Zen Buddhist teacher—a prime example of Moon in Pisces in the sixth house.

Ascendant, or Social Mask a q u s 1
Virgo: the humble servant, logical organizer, careful wordsmith, devotee, striving for simplicity and purity

With his Ascendant in Virgo, we can see that Cohen seemed humble upon first impression. He came across as reserved, with a tidy and meticulous appearance, and a critical eye.

STEP 3: THE INNER PLANETS

While the Sun, Moon, and Ascendant tell us about basic traits and emotional make-up, the inner planets expose further personal layers. In Cohen's chart, we see that his Mercury is in Libra; his Venus is in Virgo; and his Mars is in Leo. What does this mean?

Mercury, or Mind and Communication
Libra: the artist and romantic   Sag

Cohen's Mercury, or planet of communication, falls in Libra, sign of art, beauty, love, and romance. This tells us that a halo of beauty would surround his words, that he is poetically inclined, and that he had a way with expressing love through language. Known as one of the best lyricists of all time, whose poetry and often-romantic music still captivates many hearts, we can confirm this to be true.

MERCURY'S HOUSE PLACEMENT   10
First house: basic expression

The first house is the most important of all the houses. Any planets falling in this house are thusly emphasized. Here, we can see that for Cohen, communication, writing, and mental pursuits were highlighted in his life and being. We know that his identity was largely tied into being a poet and a songwriter, correlating with this house placement.

Venus, or Creativity and Romantic Nature   Cap
Virgo: the purist and perfectionist

Cohen's Venus falls in Virgo. This tells us that his creativity and romantic nature are exacting and verbal. Virgo, after all, is ruled by Mercury, planet of communication. Virgo is discerning and loyal, which would apply to Cohen's love life, creativity, style, and aesthetics. We know that he was unmarried most of his life, but at heart he stayed true to his dear Marianne, who he famously wrote about. After she died, he soon followed. In terms of aesthetics and style, we know that he wore suits every day, always uplifted and put together. This was true Venus in Virgo fashion.

However, looking at his chart, we can also see that his Venus in Virgo is conjunct Neptune, ruler of Pisces. Here lies one of Cohen's paradoxes: he is both precise and verbal in his creative expression (Venus in Virgo) and mystical and elusive as he channels his music and lyrics from another realm (Venus conjunct Neptune).

A recurring theme has shown up in Cohen's chart, which should be noted. He has a strong tendency both toward service, devotion, and language (Virgo/sixth house) and music, imagination, and mysticism (Pisces).

VENUS'S HOUSE PLACEMENT | 2

Twelfth house: the unconscious and spirituality

Venus in the twelfth house reveals a deep, unconscious drive to be loved. It can also indicate secret affairs, a dreamy and imaginative creative nature, and a desire to blend spirituality, art, and romance. We know that Cohen had many lovers, that he was certainly imaginative, and called on his spirituality as the source of much of his music and writing.

Mars, or Physical Exertion and Sexuality (Libva)

Leo: the self-expressive performer and entertainer

Here lies another dimension of Cohen's personality, beneath his restrained and precise Virgoan traits. His Mars, planet of initiative, physical exertion, and sexuality, falls in the creative, expressive sign of Leo. While his outer demeanor might be shy and humble, this indicated, accurately, that he was also a natural performer who possessed a warm and demonstrative sexual nature.

MARS'S HOUSE PLACEMENT

Eleventh house: humanitarianism and idealism

A Mars in Leo in the eleventh house reveals that Cohen applied his creative drives toward humanitarian and idealistic purposes. He was driven to think in terms of the future and the collective. We know that he wrote political songs and that he donated money to humanitarian causes, corresponding with these placements.

STEP 4: THE ASPECTS

Now that we understand Cohen's basic personality, energies, drives, and focuses, we can see how these elements relate to one another by looking at the aspects, or angles, between his planets. For now, let's focus on a few of the major aspects involving his personal planets, beginning with the most important:

Sun Conjunct Ascendant
(0°)

Whenever a planet conjuncts one of the angular house cusps, it is significant, and the Ascendant is the most powerful of the four (see chapter 9). We already know that Cohen's Sun is on his Ascendant, and that his Sun and Ascendant even fall at the exact same degree—27° Virgo.

We also know that conjunctions are the strongest aspect between two planets or points, emphasizing the energy of each. In addition, we know that the Ascendant is the most defining line in our chart, representing our outermost layer and entry point into our lives and being. And finally, we know that our Sun is our basic expression and the most powerful indicator of who we are. So how do we weave all of these elements together?

This conjunction signifies someone who makes a strong impression. Cohen would likely be a natural leader who frequently finds himself at the center of attention. It would be hard to get away with anything, because all eyes would fall on him when he walks into a room.

The Sun's natural radiance would beam through his outermost expression. In particular, his Virgoan qualities would be strong and apparent.

As a very influential singer and songwriter who garnered much fame and attention, we know all of these things to be quite true of Cohen.

Moon Opposite Venus/Neptune
(180°)

An opposition between two planets creates tension and is considered the most disharmonious angle. However, it also generates creative friction and intrigue. Moon opposite Venus and Neptune in Cohen's chart would mean that his soul and emotional self (Moon) were in dynamic conversation with both his creativity and love nature (Venus) and his dreaminess and spirituality (Neptune).

This could mean that he channeled his sensitive emotional nature (Pisces Moon) into his art and music (Venus and Neptune). It could also mean that his own personal feelings were at odds with his relationships, that it was difficult to find a balance between his deepest emotional needs and his creativity or relationships. There could even be an extreme pendulum swing between these two polarities. We know that it was difficult for Cohen to settle with one person romantically and that he left his career at one point to live in a Zen Buddhist monastery. These are strong potential manifestations of this opposition.

Mercury Trine Saturn
(120°)

Mercury trine Saturn is a common aspect in the charts of authors, songwriters, and poets, because it indicates an ability to apply the mind and communication abilities (Mercury) to career-oriented pursuits, harnessing the power of Saturn's persistence, perseverance, order, and discipline. Language would be methodical and tendencies toward perfectionism are heightened. This seems spot on for Cohen.

Aspect Patterns: T-Square

Next, let's see if Leonard Cohen has any aspect patterns, or significant shapes formed by planets in his chart. It looks like Cohen has a T-Square, or right triangle. His T-Square is formed by an opposition between Jupiter and Uranus, which are both squaring Pluto.

We know that T-Squares represent life struggles as well as great achievements, and that natives resolve their inner tension through the focal point of their T-Square. In Cohen's case, this is Pluto in Cancer in the tenth house. This means he directs tremendous energy toward a powerful emotional expression (Pluto in Cancer), which he offers to the public and his career (tenth house).

As a songwriter, Cohen created emotionally powerful songs that achieved great influence and recognition, so Cohen's T-Square was quite evident in his life and being.

SUMMARY OF LEONARD COHEN'S CHART

While Cohen's chart includes many other important features, this reading is a good beginning. Deepening your studies, you will discover more elements to look for and what they mean. But understanding these basic building blocks and following these steps, you will be able to read a chart.

Even if you only focus on the Sun, Moon, and Ascendant, and nothing else, you would be able to speak about a person's basic personality, drives, and emotional nature. There is always more to learn, but for now we can keep it simple.

INTERPRETING YOUR
OWN NATAL CHART

Now you can pull up your own chart, and we can follow the steps to interpret it. There are many free chart generators online, and I recommend using astro.com. Find the natal chart option and type in your birth data.

STEP 1: CHART EMPHASIS

First take a look at where most of your planets fall, or if they're evenly dispersed throughout your chart. If they're mostly in one quadrant, what does that say about you? You can use a journal to write down your answers.

Here is the meaning of each quadrant:

- **Eastern Hemisphere (Left Side):** self-motivating, independent, and assertive

- **Western Hemisphere (Right Side):** relationship-oriented and receptive

- **Northern Hemisphere (Bottom Half):** introverted, personal, orienting toward self-improvement and development

- **Southern Hemisphere (Top Half):** social and extroverted, oriented toward the collective and the public domain

STEP 2: THE SUN, MOON, AND ASCENDANT

Sign Placements

Now find your Sun (☉), Moon (☽), and Ascendant (AC, the line on the very left). If you don't know what time you were born, you can skip the

Ascendant. You'll still have plenty to look at. See what signs your Sun, Moon, and Ascendant fall in.

As a reminder, here are all the signs and their symbols:

Aries	Taurus	Gemini	Cancer
Leo	Virgo	Libra	Scorpio
Sagittarius	Capricorn	Aquarius	Pisces

Now you can go back to the Sun, Moon, and Ascendant chapters to look up your placement. Try to answer the following questions about each. You can write them down in a journal to help you remember:

SUN SIGN

What is your Sun sign? What does your Sun sign say about your basic expression? Your gifts and your struggles? Does it match what you know about yourself?

MOON SIGN

What is your Moon sign? What does your Moon sign say about your emotional nature? What brings you contentment according to your Moon sign? See if it matches what you know about yourself.

ASCENDANT SIGN

In which sign does your Ascendant fall? What does your Ascendant tell you about your outer expression, the first impression that you make, and your style? Does it resonate with what you know about yourself? Try asking friends how they perceived you when you first met.

House Placements

Next, see which houses your Sun and Moon fall into (if a planet falls at the very end of a house, we typically interpret it in the following house). Again, you can write down your answers to the following questions.

First, here is a reminder of the meaning of each house:

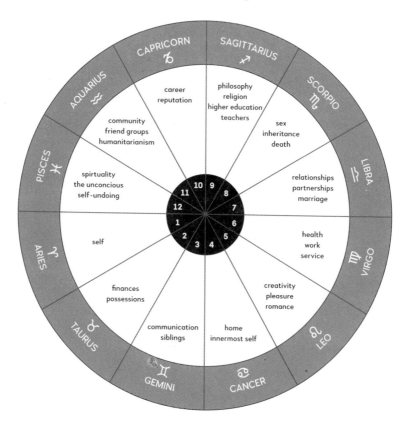

SUN HOUSE

In which house does your Sun fall? According to this placement, where do you direct your basic expression? Does your vitality depend on this area of life? See if it matches what you know about yourself.

MOON HOUSE

In which house does your Moon fall? According to this placement, where do you direct your emotional energies? Does your contentment depend on this area of life? See if it matches what you know about yourself.

STEP 3: INNER PLANETS

Look and see which signs your Mercury, Venus, and Mars fall into. You can look up their meaning in chapter 5. Write down your answers to the following questions:

Sign Placements

MERCURY SIGN

What is your Mercury sign? What does your Mercury sign say about your communication style? According to your Mercury sign, how do you speak, absorb information, and what are you likely to study? See if this matches what you know about yourself.

VENUS SIGN

What is your Venus sign? What does your Venus sign say about your love nature and personal style? According to your Venus sign, how do you love, what are your values, and how do you relate to creativity? See if it matches what you know about yourself.

MARS SIGN

What is your Mars sign? What does your Mars sign say about your impulses, sexuality, and attractions? Where do you supposedly exert yourself? See if it matches what you know about yourself.

House Placements

Next, see which houses your inner planets fall into. Write down your answers to the following questions:

MERCURY HOUSE

In which house does your Mercury fall? Where do you apply your mental energies according to your Mercury's house placement? See if it resonates with what you know about yourself.

VENUS HOUSE

In which house does your Venus fall? Where do you direct your love and creativity according to your Venus's house placement? See if it resonates with what you know about yourself.

MARS HOUSE

In which house does your Mars fall? Where do you direct your exertion according to your Mars's house placement? What area of life supposedly drives you? See if it resonates with what you know about yourself.

STEP 4: THE ASPECTS

Identify which aspects, or angles, appear in your chart. These are the blue and red lines if you're looking at your chart on astro.com.

Conjunctions
0°, or within 10° of each other

First see if there are any conjunctions, or planets falling within 10° of each other. Recalling the meaning of the planets that form the conjunction, do these energies work in tandem in your life? Examples: If your Venus (love nature) is conjunct your Sun (basic expression), are you powerfully artistic, social, or stylish? If your Moon (emotional nature) is conjunct your Mars (anger, sexuality), are your emotions laced with intense passions?

Trines
120°, or within 9° of that in either direction

Now see if you have any trines in your chart. (These are the longer blue lines on astro.com.) The energies of the planets forming a trine would work together very easily for you. Consider the significance of the planets involved, and ask yourself: Do these energies blend harmoniously in my life?

Oppositions
180°, or within 9° of that in either direction

See if you have any planets opposing each other in your chart. (These are the longest red lines on astro.com.) Knowing the meaning of the planets involved in your opposition, ask yourself: Do these energies form friction within me? Do I struggle with harmonizing these polarities in my life? Does this opposition generate dynamic creativity and passion?

Squares
90°, or within 9° of that in either direction

Finally, see if you have any squares in your chart. Knowing the meaning of the planets involved, ask yourself: Is this where I struggle in my life? Have these obstacles and challenges led me to my biggest growth lessons? Is this friction what generates intrigue, building my character and depth?

You can repeat the same process for the minor aspects.

Next, notice if you have any major aspect patterns. Are your planets forming a Grand Trine (an equilateral triangle), a T-Square (a right triangle), or a Grand Cross (a square)? Are three or more planets in a single sign or house (a Stellium)?

Here is a reminder of the major aspect patterns and their significance:

Grand Trine: An equilateral triangle, representing an easy flow of energies and natural gifts, sometimes accompanied by complacency. You can also see if all of the planets in the Grand Trine fall in a single element.

> **Fire Grand Trine:** gifts of inspiration or physical abilities.
> **Earth Grand Trine:** gifts of stability, grounding, pragmatism, and sensuality.
> **Air Grand Trine:** gifts pertaining to the mind and communication.
> **Water Grand Trine:** spiritual, intuitive, or emotional gifts.

T-Square: A right triangle, representing powerful struggle and drive.

Grand Cross: A square, representing strong gifts, accompanied by great struggle and inflexibility.

Stellium: A group of three or more planets that fall in a single house or sign, bringing great emphasis to these tendencies or this area of life.

CONTINUING YOUR ASTROLOGICAL JOURNEY

Congratulations! You've now read your own chart. As you continue to study and practice astrology, you will find that there are many more elements to learn. It is a process that can continue for the rest of your life. However, you now have a solid foundation that you can return to again and again. In fact, reading as many charts as possible is the best way to learn astrology.

Once you've mastered the fundamentals outlined in this book, the next steps could be learning about:

- The North and South Nodes, which represent our true life path and past-life or habitual tendencies

- Relationship astrology (synastry and composite charts), which show us how our natal planets interact with other people, reflecting our compatibility

- Chiron, a comet, which represents the "wounded healer," or the place in our chart that signifies our childhood wounds and where we become the healer

- Asteroids, some of which are big enough to influence our charts, including Ceres, Juno, Pallas Athena, Lilith, and Vesta

- Transits, or how the current planetary positions affect us personally, or as a collective

In the meantime, you have much to marinate in. The fundamentals of astrology are enough to allow you to read charts and glean limitless understanding. You can apply these principles to anyone you meet—partners, friends, coworkers, or family members who fascinate or perplex you. You now have a magical key to open portals of insight and wisdom.

I hope you've enjoyed this journey into the ancient art of astrology. May you continue your studies and engage in your life with heightened self-awareness, a deeper understanding of human nature, and a mind more expanded to the possibility that we are all cosmic beings—both earthly and endlessly vast.

ACKNOWLEDGMENTS

I want to extend deep gratitude to everyone who has helped to create this book. Foremost, thank you to Sara Bercholz and Juree Sondker for giving me this opportunity and for guiding me along the way, Audra Figgins for her edits, and everyone else at Roost Books and Shambhala Publications. Equally, I want to thank my dear friend and illustrator, Alejandro Cardenas, who created the extraordinary images for this book—with incredible passion, cosmic connection, and attention to detail. He has brought this book to life, imbuing it with dimensionality, magic, and myth. It has been such a joy to work with him. As two Virgos with Aquarius Moons—two mystical nerds—our pairing for this project has felt like kismet.

Next, I want to acknowledge my wonderful astrology teacher, Kelly Lee Phipps, who is no longer with us. He wasn't able to finish his own astrology book before passing away, and I've felt the writing of my own book to be a task of love for him. His spirit has continued to channel through me.

I would also like to express gratitude to my Buddhist teacher, Sakyong Mipham Rinpoche, whose wisdom, teachings, vision, and love have inspired me greatly, and Bernard Weitzman, who sparked my spiritual path with his outrageous intelligence, humor, sanity, insistence, and devotion.

Ezra Woods and Alia Raza deserve their own paragraph. They have been hugely instrumental to my astrological path, encouraging me to write regularly and orient my language toward nature, poetry, and art. I created my website, etherealculture.com, and Instagram feed, @etherealculture, after they asked me to write a monthly astrology column for their company, Régime des Fleurs (regimedesfleurs.com). I am in constant awe of their originality, style, and creativity.

Finally, thank you to all of my friends who have read drafts, helped me edit, and generally supported me—Michael Hornburg, Bonnie Hoffman, Roe Ethridge, John Searcy, Genevieve Waltcher, Jennie Rindler, and Amanda Stark-Rankins in particular.

To everyone else who has supported and inspired me who I haven't mentioned—family, friends, teachers, muses, clients, readers, and protectors —thank you.

Love to you all. May our efforts be of benefit.

GLOSSARY OF ASTROLOGICAL TERMS

Affinity: A mutual attraction between signs.

Affliction: A disharmonious aspect between two planets in a birth chart, which can cause tension or difficulty.

Air: One of the four elements, or triplicities, in which the zodiac signs are classified, along with fire, earth, and water. In astrology, air represents intellect and communication. The air signs are Gemini, Libra, and Aquarius.

Angles: *See* **Aspects**

Angular House Cusps: *See* **Aspects**

Aquarius (♒): The eleventh sign of the zodiac, which the Sun transits from January 20 to February 18. Aquarius is a fixed air sign, symbolized by the Water Bearer and ruled by the planet Uranus. Aquarius natives are innovative, original, humanitarian, and progressive.

Aries (♈): The first sign of the zodiac, which the Sun transits from March 21 to April 19. Aries is a cardinal fire sign, symbolized by the Ram and ruled by the planet Mars. Aries natives are decisive leaders, headstrong, and energetic.

Ascendant (also known as **Rising Sign**): The zodiac sign that is on the easternmost horizon at the time of birth. It is also the exact degree of the easternmost horizon at the time of birth. The Ascendant begins the first house and indicates a person's outermost layers, including physical appearance and first impressions.

Aspects (also known as **Angular House Cusps** or **Angles**): The four cardinal points in a horoscope that mark the horizon and meridian. The four aspects are the Ascendant, the Nadir (Imum Coeli), the Descendant, and the Midheaven (Medium Coeli). These are the most significant and karmic points in a birth chart. If planets fall on or near these aspects, they are emphasized in a person's personality and life.

Aspect Patterns: Specific patterns involving three or more planets or points in a chart. These are helpful to recognize when first reading a chart. Some examples:

> **Grand Cross:** A square, representing strong gifts, accompanied by great struggle and inflexibility.

Grand Trine: An equilateral triangle, representing an easy flow of energies and natural gifts, sometimes accompanied by complacency.

Stellium: A group of three or more planets that fall in a single house or sign, bringing great emphasis to these tendencies or this area of life.

T-Square: A right triangle, representing powerful struggle and drive.

Asteroids: Minor planets, new to astrology, only discovered in the nineteenth century. Some are believed to have significant astrological influence, particularly Ceres, Pallas, Juno, Vesta, and Lilith. We are still at the beginning stages of exploring and considering the asteroids in Western astrology.

Astrology (comes from the Greek word *astrologia*, meaning "the study of the stars"): The study of celestial bodies and their positions and movements to determine aspects of human affairs and the natural world.

Birth Chart (also known as **Natal Chart**): A horoscope or map of celestial bodies that indicates the planetary positions at the time of birth. When interpreted, the birth chart reveals facets of who we are, such as our personality, character, gifts, struggles, and purpose.

Cancer (♋): The fourth sign of the zodiac, which the Sun transits from June 21 to July 22. Cancer is a cardinal water sign, symbolized by the Crab and ruled by the Moon. Cancer natives are emotional, imaginative, sensitive, nurturing, and moody.

Capricorn (♑): The tenth sign of the zodiac, which the Sun transits from December 22 to January 19. Capricorn is a cardinal earth sign, symbolized by the Sea-Goat and ruled by the planet Saturn. Capricorn natives are ambitious, disciplined, traditional, and responsible, with ample integrity.

Cardinal: One of the three qualities, or quadruplicities, in which the zodiac signs are classified. The three qualities are cardinal, fixed, and mutable. The cardinal signs fall at the beginning of each season: Aries in spring, Cancer in summer, Libra in fall, and Capricorn in winter. The cardinal signs are leaders and idea people, possessing qualities of initiative, enthusiasm, and inspiration.

Chiron: A planet discovered in 1977, that has a unique and erratic orbit. Most Western astrologers consider and interpret its placement. Symbolized by the Wounded Healer, Chiron points to our childhood wounds. It also reflects how we become the healer as we resolve our deepest pain and feelings of inadequacy.

Conjunction: The most powerful aspect between two planets in a horoscope, where they fall at the same degree or within 10° of each other. The planetary energies merge and emphasize each other.

Constellations: Groups of stars that form patterns, which were named by the ancients. The zodiac signs correlate with constellations.

Cusp: The point at which a sign of the zodiac begins. When people are born close to the beginning or end of a sign, they are born on the cusp, demonstrating characteristics of both signs.

Descendant: One of the four angles, or angular house cusps, in a horoscope. The Descendant marks the cusp of the seventh house, directly opposite the Ascendant. This line represents our shadow and how we relate to partnerships and marriage.

Duality: One of the classifications of the zodiac signs. A sign's duality is either masculine or feminine. The feminine signs are Taurus, Cancer, Virgo, Scorpio, Capricorn, and Pisces. The masculine signs are Aries, Gemini, Leo, Libra, Sagittarius, and Aquarius. Feminine signs are receptive and oriented toward the inner world. Masculine signs are energetic, action-based, and oriented toward the outer world.

Earth: 1. One of the four elements, or triplicities, in which zodiac signs are classified, along with fire, water, and air. In astrology, earth represents practicality and stability. The earth signs are Taurus, Virgo, and Capricorn.

2. (When capitalized): The planet that we inhabit.

Ecliptic: The circle in the cosmos that represents the Sun's apparent path from Earth. In reality, the Earth revolves around the Sun, but the ecliptic describes the path of the Sun from the perspective of Earth.

Elements: The four basic substances on Earth, which correspond with classifications of the zodiac signs: fire, earth, air, and water. Fire signs are inspiring and energetic; earth signs are practical and stable; air signs are intellectual and communicative; water signs are emotional and imaginative.

Equinoxes (Spring and Fall): The two points in the year when the Sun crosses the celestial equator, making day and night equal in length. The spring or vernal equinox occurs when the Sun enters Aries. The fall or autumnal equinox occurs when the Sun enters Libra.

Fire: One of the four elements, or triplicities, in which zodiac signs are classified, along with earth, water, and air. In astrology, fire represents inspiration, enthusiasm, and impulsiveness. The fire signs are Aries, Leo, and Sagittarius.

Fixed: One of the three qualities, or quadruplicities, in which the zodiac signs are classified. The three qualities are cardinal, fixed, and mutable. The fixed signs fall in the middle of each season. They are Taurus, Leo, Scorpio, and Aquarius. The fixed signs are the stabilizers, who are steady, purposeful, and also rigid or stubborn.

Gemini (♊): The third sign of the zodiac, which the Sun transits from May 21 to June 20. Gemini is a mutable air sign, symbolized by the Twins and ruled by the planet Mercury. Gemini natives are intellectual, curious, mercurial, and communicative.

Glyphs: The typographical symbols that represent each planet or sign. A uniform set of symbols is contained within the glyphs. For example, the circle represents the spiritual world; the half circle represents the soul; and the cross represents the material world.

Grand Configurations: *See* **Aspect Patterns**

Hellenistic Astrology: A tradition of Greco-Roman astrology that originated around the first century B.C.E., merging ancient Babylonian and Egyptian astrology after the Alexandrian conquests in Egypt. It is the origin of much of modern astrology practiced today.

Hemispheric Emphasis: Where the predominance of planets fall along the circular horoscope, divided into four hemispheres—top, bottom, left, and right, or south, north, east, and west. Many planets in the top hemisphere represent extroversion; the bottom is introversion; the left indicates assertiveness; the right indicates receptivity.

Horizon: The line in a horoscope that divides the circle east to west, connecting the Ascendant and Descendant.

Horoscope (from the Greek words *hora*, meaning "hour," and *skopos*, meaning "watcher"): A diagram of the ecliptic, divided into twelve parts, known as houses, that indicates the positions of the Sun, Moon, and planets in relation to a particular place on Earth. The word *horoscope* can also refer to the interpretation of this chart, in addition to predictions of upcoming energies for an individual or the collective.

Houses: The twelve divisions of a horoscope that represent different categories of life. This is the area of life where we apply the energies of our planets. There are many different housing systems that astrologers adhere to. The one most commonly used (and the one used in this book) is the Placidus system.

Imum Coeli: *See* **Nadir**

Jupiter (♃): The planet of good fortune, expansion, wisdom, and abundance.

Karma: A notion originating in Hinduism and Buddhism that our previous actions affect our future existence. This notion is strongly tied to modern astrology, with the prevalent understanding that our soul's karma matches the positions of planets at the moment of birth, unlocking our spiritual journey in this lifetime.

Leo (♌): The fifth sign of the zodiac, which the Sun transits from July 23 to August 22. Leo is a fixed fire sign, symbolized by the Lion and ruled by the Sun. Leo natives are creative, expressive, warm, and self-centered.

Libra (♎): The seventh sign of the zodiac, which the Sun transits from September 23 to October 22. Libra is a cardinal air sign, symbolized by the Scales and ruled by the planet Venus. Libra natives are harmonious, artistic, romantic, and indecisive.

Mars (♂): The planet of physical exertion, sexuality, and aggression.

Medium Coeli: *See* **Midheaven**

Mercury (☿): The planet of the mind, intellect, and communication.

Meridian: The line in a horoscope that divides the circle north to south, connecting the Nadir and the Midheaven.

Midheaven (also known as Medium Coeli, abbreviated as MC, meaning "highest part of the heavens"): One of the four angles, or angular house cusps, in a horoscope. The Midheaven marks the cusp of the tenth house, directly opposite the Nadir. This line represents ambition, career, and public image.

Moon (☽): The "planet" or luminary that represents our emotions, sensitivity, and subconscious.

Mundane Astrology: The branch of astrology that pertains to world events, politics, natural phenomena, and historical cycles.

Mutable: One of the three qualities, or quadruplicities, in which the zodiac signs are classified. The three qualities are cardinal, fixed, and mutable. The mutable signs fall at the end of each season. They are Gemini, Virgo, Sagittarius, and Pisces. The mutable signs are adaptable, sympathetic, and have a go-with-the-flow nature.

Nadir (also known as Imum Coeli, abbreviated as IC, meaning "lowest part of the heavens"): One of the four angles, or angular house cusps, in a horoscope. The Nadir marks the cusp of the fourth house, directly opposite the

Midheaven. This line represents a person's deepest, most intimate layers, including the home, the nurturing parent, and the inner world.

Natal Chart: *See* **Birth Chart**

Native: A person born with a particular planetary placement. For example, if we are talking about someone who has Mercury in Aquarius in her natal chart, we would refer to her as a Mercury-in-Aquarius native.

Neptune (Ψ): The planet of spirituality, compassion, illusion, imagination, and transcendence.

Nodes: The North and South Nodes are points directly opposite each other that form the Nodal axis. They are the points where the Moon's orbit intersects the plane of the ecliptic. Our spiritual journey involves balancing our North and South Nodes, or the area in our chart that they represent. We must bring the natural gifts of our South Node to the path of the North Node.

> **North Node:** The area of our life where we must exert ourselves in order to grow spiritually. This is often a place of discomfort in our chart, as well as the biggest source of potential growth. It represents our life's true purpose.

> **South Node:** Our past lives, what comes most naturally to us, and where our habituations pull us back.

Opposition (☍): A major aspect, in which two planets or points oppose each other in a birth chart, forming a 180° angle, or within 9° of that in either direction. Traditionally, this is considered to be a disharmonious aspect, creating friction and challenges. While challenging, it is a source of potential growth, drive, dynamism, and achievement.

Orbit: The path of any celestial body as it revolves around another celestial body.

Part of Fortune (also known by its Latin name, *Pars Fortuna*): A point in a birth chart in which the longitude of the Ascendant is added to the longitude of the Moon, and then subtracted by the longitude of the Sun. Modern astrologers consider this point to be an area of success and good fortune in a person's life.

Pisces (♓): The twelfth sign of the zodiac, which the Sun transits from February 19 to March 20. Pisces is a mutable water sign, symbolized by the Fish and ruled by the planet Neptune. Pisces natives are sensitive, spiritual, impressionable, and compassionate. As the last sign of the zodiac, it encompasses all the signs that came before.

Planet (from the Greek word *planets*, meaning "wanderer"): A celestial body moving around a star. In astrology, planets refer to the celestial bodies moving around the Sun, in addition to the Sun and Moon.

Pluto (♇): The planet of surrender, transformation, and power.

Polarity (also known as **Polar Opposite**): Opposite zodiac signs, for example, Aries and Libra, or Taurus and Scorpio.

Progressed Chart: An ancient method of casting a horoscope that reveals the phase of life we are in. One day equals one year of life, so the horoscope for the day after you were born would represent your second year of life. The most important progressions are when your natal Sun or Moon move into the next sign.

Quadrant (from the Latin word *quadrans*, meaning "fourth"): One of the four quarters of a horoscopic circle. Each quadrant contains three houses and holds a different meaning.

Quadruplicity: A group of four astrological signs that belongs to the same quality—either cardinal, fixed, or mutable. The cardinal quadruplicity includes Aries, Cancer, Libra, and Capricorn; the fixed quadruplicity includes Taurus, Leo, Scorpio, and Aquarius; the mutable quadruplicity includes Gemini, Virgo, Sagittarius, and Pisces.

Qualities: The three types of energies in which the signs are classified. The three qualities are cardinal, fixed, and mutable. Cardinal signs are initiating; fixed signs are stabilizing; mutable signs are adaptable.

Quincunx (⚻): A minor angle, in which two or more planets or points form a 150° angle in a birth chart, or within 2° of that in either direction. The quincunx is mildly disharmonious. The two energies cannot merge.

Rising Sign: *See* **Ascendant**

Ruler (also known as **Ruling Planet**): 1. The planet that has dominion over a certain zodiac sign. For example, Mercury rules Gemini and Virgo; the Sun rules Leo.

2. In a birth chart, the planet that rules the Ascendant is said to be the ruling planet of the chart. The ruling planet holds particular significance for the individual.

Sagittarius (♐): The ninth sign of the zodiac, which the Sun transits from November 22 to December 22. Sagittarius is a mutable air sign, symbolized by the Archer and ruled by the planet Jupiter. Sagittarius natives are philosophical, optimistic, and zealous, and love travel, freedom, and adventure.

Saturn (♄): The planet of responsibility, ambition, society, and tradition.

Scorpio (♏): The eighth sign of the zodiac, which the Sun transits from October 23 to November 21. Scorpio is a fixed water sign, symbolized by the Scorpion and ruled by the planets Pluto and Mars. Scorpio natives are possessive, deep, powerful, intense, and probing.

Semisextile (⚹): A minor aspect, in which two or more planets or points form a 30° angle in a birth chart, or within 2° of that in either direction. Mildly harmonious, it is a less powerful version of the sextile.

Semisquare (∠): A minor aspect, in which two or more planets or points form a 45° angle in a birth chart, or within 2° of that in either direction. Mildly disharmonious, it is a less powerful version of the square.

Sesquisquare (⚼): A minor aspect, in which two or more planets or points are 135° apart in a birth chart, or within 2° of that in either direction. Mildly disharmonious, its effects are similar to a semisquare.

Sextile (⚹): A major aspect, in which two or more planets or points in a chart are 60° apart, or within 6° of that in either direction. This is considered a harmonious aspect, the energies blending easily and supporting each other.

Signs of the Zodiac (also known as **Astrological Signs**): The twelve 30° segments of the zodiac wheel, based on the path of constellations through which the Sun travels from the perspective of Earth. The twelve signs are: Aries, Taurus, Gemini, Cancer, Leo, Virgo, Libra, Scorpio, Sagittarius, Capricorn, Aquarius, and Pisces.

Solstices (Summer and Winter): The two points in the year when the Sun is farthest from the celestial equator. The summer solstice occurs when the Sun enters Cancer; this is the longest day of the year. The winter solstice occurs when the Sun enters Capricorn; this is the shortest day of the year.

Square (□): A major aspect, in which two or more planets or points in an astrological chart are 90° apart, or within 9° of that in either direction. A disharmonious aspect, it indicates challenges for the native that ultimately lead to growth, drive, and development of character.

Sun (☉): The "planet" or luminary that represents our emotions, sensitivity, and subconscious.

Taurus (♉): The second sign of the zodiac, which the Sun transits from April 20 to May 20. Taurus is a fixed earth sign, symbolized by the Bull and ruled by the planet Venus. Taurus natives are sensual, trustworthy, stubborn, and earthy.

Transit: The passage of a planet through a sign or position in a horoscope.

Trine (△): A major aspect, in which two or more planets or points in an astrological chart are 120° apart, or within 9° of that in either direction. A trine is the most harmonious aspect in astrology, where the two energies support each other fluidly. Trines generate natural contentment and even complacency because of their ease.

Triplicity: A group of three astrological signs that belong to the same element. The fire triplicity includes Aries, Leo, and Sagittarius; the earth triplicity includes Taurus, Virgo, and Capricorn; the air triplicity includes Gemini, Libra, and Aquarius; the water triplicity includes Cancer, Scorpio, and Pisces.

Uranus (♅): The planet of intuition, rebellion, and revolution.

Venus (♀): The planet of love, creativity, and values.

Virgo (♍): The sixth sign of the zodiac, which the Sun transits from August 23 to September 22. Virgo is a mutable earth sign, symbolized by the Virgin and ruled by the planet Mercury. Virgo natives are devoted, service-oriented, meticulous, and critical.

Water: One of the four elements, or triplicities, in which zodiac signs are classified, along with fire, earth, and air. In astrology, water represents emotions, sensitivity, imagination, and spirituality. The water signs are Cancer, Scorpio, and Pisces.

Western Astrology: The system of astrology popular in Western countries. The system is based on Ptolemy's *Tetrabiblos* from the second century C.E., which was a continuation of Hellenistic astrology.

Zodiac (from the Greek word *zodiakos*, meaning "circle of animals"): A band circling the Earth, just above and below the ecliptic, which contains constellations and the planets that orbit the Sun, except for Pluto. The zodiac is a perfect 360° circle, divided into twelve signs that correlate with the constellations: Aries, Taurus, Gemini, Cancer, Leo, Virgo, Libra, Scorpio, Sagittarius, Capricorn, Aquarius, and Pisces. While the constellations are different sizes, the twelve signs of the zodiac are 30° each.

BIBLIOGRAPHY

Arroyo, Steve, *Chart Interpretation Handbook*. Sebastopol, CA: CRCS Publications, 2015.

Campbell, Joseph, and Bill Moyers. *The Power of Myth*. Norwell, MA: Anchor, 1991.

Cunningham, Donna. *An Astrological Guide to Self-Awareness*. Sebastopol, CA: CRCS Publications, 1978.

Forrest, Steven. *The Inner Sky: How to Make Wiser Choices for a More Fulfilling Life*. Portland, OR: Seven Paws Press, 2007.

——. *The Book of Pluto: Finding Wisdom in Darkness*. Portland, OR: Seven Paws Press, 2012.

——. *The Book of Neptune*. Portland, OR: Seven Paws Press, 2016.

Gettings, Fred. *The Arkana Dictionary of Astrology*. New York: Penguin Group, 1990.

Goodman, Linda. *Linda Goodman's Sun Signs*. New York: Bantam Books, 1985.

Greene, Liz, and Robert Hand. *Saturn: A New Look at an Old Devil*. Newburyport, MA: Weiser Books, 2011.

Greene, Liz, and Howard Sasportas. *The Luminaries: The Psychology of the Sun and Moon in the Horoscope*. Newburyport, MA: Weiser Books, 1992.

——. *The Inner Planets: Building Blocks of Personal Reality*. Newburyport, MA: Weiser Books, 1993.

Hand, Robert. *Horoscope Symbols*. Gloucester, MA: Para Research, 1981.

Hickey, Isabel. *Astrology, A Cosmic Science: The Classic Work on Spiritual Astrology*. Sebastopol, CA: CRCS Publications, 2011.

Howell, Alice O. *Jungian Symbolism in Astrology*. Wheaton, IL: The Theosophical Publishing House, 1987.

Jung, C. G. Edited by Violet S. de Laszlo. *Psyche and Symbol*. Garden City, NY: Doubleday and Company, 1958.

——. *Synchronicity: An Acausal Connecting Principle*. New York: Pantheon Books, 1955.

Lachman, Gary. *Jung the Mystic: The Esoteric Dimensions of Carl Jung's Life and Teachings*. New York: TarcherPerigee, 2012.

Mayo, Jeff. *The Astrologer's Astronomical Handbook*. Essex, England: L. N. Fowler & Co., 1982.

Oken, Alan. *Complete Astrology*. New York: Bantam Books, 1988.

Ptolemy, Claudius. Edited and translated by F. E. Robbins. *Tetrabiblos*. London: William Heinemann, 1964.

Rudhyar, Dane. *The Astrological Houses: The Spectrum of Individual Experience*. New York: Doubleday, 1972.

Sasportas, Howard. *The Twelve Houses: Exploring the Houses of the Horoscope*. London: Flare Publications, 2010.

Tester, Jim. *A History of Western Astrology*. New York: Ballantine Books, 1988.

Tompkins, Sue. *Aspects in Astrology*. Merrimac, MA: Destiny Publishers, 2002.

Woolfolk, Joanna Martine. *The Only Astrology Book You'll Ever Need*. Lanham, MD: Taylor Trade Publishing, 2012.

SUGGESTED FURTHER READING

Books

Arroyo, Steve. *Chart Interpretation Handbook*. Sebastopol, CA: CRCS Publications, 2015.

Forrest, Steven. *The Inner Sky: How to Make Wiser Choices for a More Fulfilling Life*. Portland, OR: Seven Paws Press, 2007.

———. *The Book of Pluto: Finding Wisdom in Darkness*. Portland, OR: Seven Paws Press, 2012.

———. *The Book of Neptune*. Portland, OR: Seven Paws Press, 2016.

Green, John. *Do You Love Me? The Astrology of Relationships*. England, UK: MISPA Books, 2015.

Greene, Liz. *Relationships and How to Survive Them*. CPA Press, 2013.

Greene, Liz, and Robert Hand. *Saturn: A New Look at an Old Devil*. Newburyport, MA: Weiser Books, 2011.

Greene, Liz, and Howard Sasportas. *The Luminaries: The Psychology of the Sun and Moon in the Horoscope*. Newburyport, MA: Weiser Books, 1992.

———. *The Inner Planets: Building Blocks of Personal Reality*. Newburyport, MA: Weiser Books, 1993.

Hand, Robert. *Planets in Transit: Life Cycles for Living*. Atglen, PA: Schiffer Publishing, Ltd., 2001.

Hickey, Isabel. *Astrology, A Cosmic Science: The Classic Work on Spiritual Astrology*. Sebastopol, CA: CRCS Publications, 2011.

Oken, Alan. *Complete Astrology*. New York: Bantam Books, 1988.

Reinhart, Melanie. *Chiron and the Healing Journey*. London: Starwalker Press, 2013.

Sasportas, Howard. *The Twelve Houses: Exploring the Houses of the Horoscope*. London: Flare Publications, 2010.

Spiller, Jan. *Astrology for the Soul*. New York: Bantam Books, 2009.

Websites

www.astro.com | www.astrologers.com | www.astrology-numerology.com
www.cafeastrology.com | www.mountainastrologer.com

INDEX

ABOUT THE AUTHOR

Juliana McCarthy has been practicing and studying astrology for almost twenty years, finding it to be a powerful tool for self-exploration and examining how we relate to others. She loves working with people and helping them understand their authentic selves—their complexities, gifts, karma, and life paths. An avid writer and lover of art, she writes articles for her website, etherealculture.com, and runs a popular Instagram feed by the same name, @etherealculture. Juliana is also an energy healer and a longtime student of Tibetan Buddhism.

ABOUT THE ILLUSTRATOR

Alejandro Cardenas is a Latin-American artist and designer. As a child, his Chilean grandmother taught him how to read tarot and opened his imagination to mythology and mysticism. In 1996, Alejandro moved to New York to study fine art at Cooper Union, and later made his name working with prints and textiles for designer Proenza Schouler. His work spans the worlds of art, fashion, design, and animation. He now lives in Los Angeles with his wife and two daughters.